Beyond the Horse Race

Beyond the Horse Race

How to Read Polls and Why We Should

JOHN ZOGBY

ROWMAN & LITTLEFIELD
Lanham • Boulder • New York • London

Published by Rowman & Littlefield
An imprint of The Rowman & Littlefield Publishing Group, Inc.
4501 Forbes Boulevard, Suite 200, Lanham, Maryland 20706
www.rowman.com

86-90 Paul Street, London EC2A 4NE

British Library Cataloguing in Publication Information Available

Library of Congress Cataloging-in-Publication Data

Names: Zogby, John, author.
Title: Beyond the horse race : how to read polls and why we should / John
    Zogby.
Description: Lanham, Maryland : Rowman & Littlefield Publishing Group,
    2024. | Includes bibliographical references and index. | Summary: "John
    Zogby, one of America's most prominent pollsters, offers readers a
    master class in understanding what polls can reveal about public
    opinion. Illustrating his arguments from key political races of the last
    40 years, Zogby shares true stories about how polls have been misused
    and when they have been well or badly"— Provided by publisher.
Identifiers: LCCN 2024014739 (print) | LCCN 2024014740 (ebook) | ISBN
    9781538197141 (cloth) | ISBN 9781538197158 (epub)
Subjects: LCSH: Election forecasting—United States. | Public opinion
    polls—United States. | United States—Politics and government—Public
    opinion.
Classification: LCC JK2007 .Z64 2024 (print) | LCC JK2007 (ebook) | DDC
    324.973—dc23/eng/20240513
LC record available at https://lccn.loc.gov/2024014739
LC ebook record available at https://lccn.loc.gov/2024014740

∞™ The paper used in this publication meets the minimum requirements of American
National Standard for Information Sciences—Permanence of Paper
for Printed Library Materials, ANSI/NISO Z39.48-1992.

To my mother, Celia Ann Zogby, the smartest person I've ever known. I've had the privilege of meeting and working with elites worldwide, and you could have held court with any of them. Sometimes you did—for example, when you went on *Good Morning, America*. After watching *Roots*, you put pen to paper and wrote out seven generations of your and Dad's families. You were counselor to four generations of us, an extraordinary middle school teacher, and you were always guided by your faith first. This one is for you, Mom.

To my mother, Celia Ann Zogby, the smartest person I've ever known. I've had the privilege of meeting and working with elites worldwide, and you could have held court with any of them. Sometimes you did—for example, when you went on *Good Morning, America*. After watching *Roots*, you put pen to paper and wrote out seven generations of your and Dad's families. You were counselor to four generations of us, an extraordinary middle school teacher, and you were always guided by your faith first. This one is for you, Mom.

Contents

Acknowledgments

It doesn't always take a village, but it sure helps to have great people standing with you. Dr. John Nader, president of the State University of New York at Farmingdale, wears the title of "muse" for this book. He called me out of the blue a few years ago and said I needed to write another book. He suggested it would be a useful contribution for me to look back at my many opinion research projects and share the lessons that my clients and I have learned over four decades of being a pollster. I got excited, and that began the process of jotting down notes on corners of junk mail envelopes, torn corners of scrap paper, and the margins of hardcopy reports from the past.

Shortly thereafter, I heard from Carole Sargent, director of scholarly publications at Georgetown University, who acts as a book developer for people like me. Carole did more than encourage me. She believed in me, even as the original idea (which is still an unpublished manuscript) evolved into a different book about how to read polls. We Zoomed many times as I wrote, she edited, I added, she suggested and sharpened. Carole was my Henry Higgins, and this work—and the original book—owe so much to her.

Carole contacted her former colleague Richard Brown of Sheed & Ward, who referred it to his colleague Jon Sisk of Rowman & Littlefield. He was very enthusiastic about my draft and wanted it for the 2024 cycle. His assistant, Mikayla Lindsay, served as point with aplomb and diligence.

Patrick McSweeney, then a graduate student in political science at Georgetown, was research assistant and saved me an enormous amount of time.

By 1996, my polling reputation and brand were on a terrific trajectory. It was at that moment, in May 1996, that I was invited to lunch in New York with Stephen Jukes, newly appointed editor of North and South America (later world news editor), and Alan Elsner, chief political and Washington correspondent for Reuters, the largest news-gathering agency in the world. Their confidence in me and my wonderful team turned into a thirteen-year professional and personal relationship filled with full support, expansion to other world hotspots, and warm friendships. I will also add Adrian Dickson, who served as Reuters's chief correspondent for Brazil and later editor for Asia, who also provided me with enormous opportunities over the years. Real professionals and good friends.

As always, Kathy, my wife of nearly a half century, has always been at my side. And two of our three our sons, Jeremy Zogby and Ben Zogby, have evolved into my colleagues, friends, and producers of beautiful grandchildren. Their wonderful wives—Marija and Nertila—made substantial contributions to the production of our babies.

Any mistakes are mine. But you know that already.

By the way, when reading the tables in this book, bear in mind that percentages (%) and frequencies (*f*) may not add up to 100 percent or completely align with the totals shown, due to rounding and weighting.

CHAPTER 1

Good Polls, Bad Polls, No Polls

My friend and polling colleague Scott Rasmussen tells a story too familiar to many of us pollsters. We have all blown a race or two over the years, and yet we also know how important we have become to reporters, pundits, and political junkies. Scott did not have his finest hour in November 2000, when his final poll results came in with Governor George W. Bush leading by nine percentage points over Vice President Al Gore. As we know, Gore won the popular vote by one half of one percentage point.[1] A reporter called Scott and asked two questions:

"What happened with your poll?"

He took about a minute to respond.

Then the reporter followed with "What have you got about 2004?" That was the next election, four years into the future.

There you have it. Folks love to hate us and poke holes in our work, but they cannot live without us. We have data and they don't.

Polls can be right or wrong in the political world, but those who focus only on the horse-race sweepstakes can miss the real utilitarian value that they provide.[2] In fact, for me the horse-race question about who is ahead and who is behind only gives us some grounding and a key to what the rest of the poll offers. And for clients (many of whom should know better) who merely want to know whether they are leading, the horse-race aspect is much too one-dimensional. They need to focus on the internals, the crosstabs (as we call them in the business), to answer questions and provide an enormous amount of detail: for example, how vulnerable an incumbent is (if there is indeed an incumbent), where there are openings, who is currently with them and against them and why, who is genuinely undecided and what can move them, how are folks doing financially, what issues are most important, which are key drivers in how a person will ultimately make a decision, and who needs to be nudged to even bother to vote. Many respondents to a poll have little or no idea where they stand politically, and thus are up for grabs, and important to introduce to the client. For example, in 1999, two years before the election in which Mike Bloomberg ran for office, why were so many New Yorkers not familiar with what kind of candidate he would be? They knew him only as a businessman.

And that is only a partial list of answers that a very modest poll can yield. There are true stories about how polls have been misused, when they have been nonexistent although truly needed, and how many have been well done by some and badly done by others. I want to tell some of these stories, especially some of those in which I was directly involved.

Consider these two different polling scenarios, both true.

Exhibit A: Good Polling versus Bad Polling— Thursday, November 2, 2000

I had just finished lecturing in a class at the Center for Politics at Harvard's Kennedy School for my friend and colleague Rick Davis, Senator John McCain's longtime strategist. My cell phone rang as I was on my way to dinner with some Kennedy Center officials. It was Ari Fleischer, communications director for candidate George W. Bush, who would go on to become the spokesman for President Bush.

"You really have this race with Gore tightening up?"

"I do."

Vice President Al Gore was starting to make gains and was, as of that afternoon, three points down.[3] In a race that I was tracking daily for Reuters and NBC News, there had been a seesaw battle all throughout October, and Gore had just been down by as much as five a few days earlier.[4]

"Well, you have it all wrong," Fleischer told me. "We have at least 54 percent in the popular vote and 320 electoral votes locked up."

"Ari, one of us will be selling pencils on the street on Wednesday morning." I must admit I was really worried it would be me!

After dinner, I turned the television on when I got to my hotel room, just in time to catch the lead story on Channel 4 in Boston. Former Texas Governor Bush, it was reported, had been arrested and charged thirty years earlier for two separate DUI incidents.[5] The story spread explosively, and those were the days when things like that mattered. We did in fact see Gore continue to make gains, particularly among women bothered by the arrests and among voters over sixty-five.[6] Remember that there had been a notable gender gap since the late 1980s, with women favoring Democratic candidates and men preferring Republicans. However, as my friend and Catholic University of America professor and author John Kenneth White pointed out, there was a substantial gap between married women, who leaned Republican, and single/divorced women, who leaned heavily Democrat.[7] In 2000, it would be married women who moved several points over to Gore late in the campaign. Table 1.1 shows just how close this was.

Table 1.1. Reuters/MSNBC/Zogby Final National Poll, November 2000

	Gender						Party					
	Total		Male		Female		Democrat		Republican		Independent	
	f	%	f	%	f	%	f	%	f	%	f	%
Gore	557	47.8	221	39.1	336	55.9	372	81.2	38	9.1	147	49.9
Bush	541	46.4	299	53.0	242	40.2	66	14.5	356	86.4	118	40.0
Buchanan	5	.5	2	.4	3	.5	2	.4	1	.2	3	.8
Nader	53	4.5	35	6.2	18	2.9	15	3.3	15	3.7	22	7.6
Browne	7	.6	6	1.0	1	.2	1	.1	2	.6	4	1.3
Hagelin	1	.1			1	.2					1	.4
Phillips												
McReynolds	2	.2	2	.3			2	.4				
NS												
Total	1166	100.0	564	100.0	602	100.0	458	100.0	412	100.0	295	100.0

	Ideology													
	Prog/Very Lib		Liberal		Moderate		Conservative		Very Cons		Libertarian		NS	
	f	%	f	%	f	%	f	%	f	%	f	%	f	%
Gore	62	70.8	174	84.2	191	50.4	67	19.4	7	14.4	6	24.3	45	68.6
Bush	13	14.4	26	12.4	158	41.8	271	78.5	42	82.8	11	42.1	20	29.5
Buchanan	1	.8			2	.6	2	.7						
Nader	11	12.7	7	3.4	22	5.8	5	1.3	1	2.8	5	20.2	1	1.9
Browne					4	.9					3	13.5		
Hagelin	1	1.3												
Phillips														
McReynolds					2	.5								
NS														
Total	88	100.0	207	100.0	379	100.0	345	100.0	50	100.0	25	100.0	66	100.0

	Age Group									
	Total		18–29		30–49		50–64		65+	
	f	%	f	%	f	%	f	%	f	%
Gore	549	47.8	100	59.0	159	44.4	154	48.8	136	44.7
Bush	531	46.3	57	33.9	170	47.4	151	47.9	153	50.2
Buchanan	5	.5	1	.8	1	.3	1	.2	2	.6
Nader	52	4.5	7	3.9	25	7.1	10	3.0	10	3.4
Browne	7	.6	4	2.3	2	.5			1	.4
Hagelin	1	.1			1	.3				
Phillips										
McReynolds	2	.2							2	.6
NS										
Total	1148	100.0	169	100.0	358	100.0	315	100.0	305	100.0

As for voters over sixty-five, the key was to understand them in historical context. When I first started polling in the 1980s, the oldest cohort of this group was those who came of age during the Depression and New Deal, loyalists to the New Deal until the end. But a new wave of seniors had their fill of the welfare state and were the so-called silent generation, or what I call the private generation.[8] They came of age during the Cold War and tended to be patriotic, conservative, and the most racist of the age cohorts. While this was a group who supported Ronald Reagan, and who were disgusted with the behavior of Bill Clinton, they were also the most loyal to Social Security, which they were now receiving.[9] They were troubled by Bush's lack of transparency over his arrests, especially since it came just after they had endured Clinton's disingenuousness. And they were also most bothered by Bush's promise to privatize at least some of Social Security.

The race was tied in our Sunday tracking, and Gore eventually, by late Monday afternoon, took the lead.[10] When *NBC Nightly News* led its broadcast Monday night with "A stunning new Zogby poll shows Vice President Al Gore taking the lead in the presidential race," I started thinking about where I could get the cheapest bulk orders for lead pencils for my next career.

However, Gore did in fact go on to win the popular vote. I guess things worked out well for both Fleischer and me.[11] There was some good polling (Zogby) and some bad polling (Fleischer). But Bush did ultimately get to the White House (bad polling, but he won).

A few days later, the night of the election, I briefed the Foreign Press Association at the Foreign Press Center in Washington, DC, with satellite connections for press in New York and London. During the briefing, I was handed a slip of paper telling me that my client, NBC News, was calling Florida for Gore and hence projecting him to win the entire election. I was flummoxed because I understood that the national popular vote was heading in the vice president's direction, but my up-to-the-minute polling had shown Gore leading in Florida by only one point! And the early network exit poll releases that were out at 1:00 p.m. showed the same one-point lead for Gore. This was definitely not enough to make a call.

A couple of hours later, I was doing a Canadian Broadcasting Company interview with Peter Baker (then of the *Washington Post*, later of the *New York Times*). We were right in the middle of explaining how Gore won when the television monitor in the newsroom displayed CNN, who with the other networks had called it for Gore, changing its declaration to Bush. Tough spot for Baker and me. We now know the rest, but the polling was very clear that both Florida and the nation were simply too close to call.

I am a registered Democrat and view my world through that lens. But I have been beloved over the years by Republicans because, as you will see, I have accurately reflected in my polls higher turnouts by Republicans. I honestly believe that Gore did in fact win Florida in 2000 and hence the election. I base this on one fact: my preelection polling showed him doing sufficiently well in south Florida, where at that time there was normally a solid Democratic vote, although things later changed. It also showed him doing better than expected in both the Republican north of the state and the "swing central," that famed I-4 corridor linking Tampa with Orlando.

Gore, of course, eked out a win in the popular vote nationwide by virtue of his light margin over Bush among moderate voters and Catholics. He did underperform—compared with Bill Clinton and Barack Obama—among Black voters, but there is no doubt that what hurt his overall chances nationally was the performance of Green Party candidate Ralph Nader, who, while scoring only a little over 2 percent in the popular vote, did much better among normally Democratic voting blocs: 7 percent among single voters and 7 percent among thirty-to-forty-nine-year-olds. Nader did particularly well with independents (8 percent).

Table 1.2. Reuters/MSNBC/Zogby Final Florida Poll, November 2000

	Total		Region							
			Panhandle		West		East		Miami	
	f	%	f	%	f	%	f	%	f	%
Gore	285	48.0	67	46.8	84	47.7	103	49.6	30	46.4
Bush	274	46.2	64	45.2	86	48.8	92	44.4	31	46.9
Buchanan	2	.3	1	.8			1	.3		
Nader	32	5.5	10	7.2	6	3.4	12	5.6	4	6.7
Total	593	100.0	143	100.0	177	100.0	208	100.0	65	100.0

	Party					
	Democrat		Republican		Independent	
	f	%	f	%	f	%
Gore	186	81.1	24	10.4	74	57.2
Bush	30	13.1	204	87.5	40	30.5
Buchanan	1	.2	1	.6		
Nader	13	5.6	4	1.5	16	12.3
Total	229	100.0	233	100.0	130	100.0

(continued)

Table 1.2.   Reuters/MSNBC/Zogby Final Florida Poll, November 2000, *Continued*

	Age Group							
	18–29		30–49		50–64		65+	
	f	%	f	%	f	%	f	%
Gore	37	48.0	87	48.3	63	38.6	92	57.3
Bush	32	41.7	83	46.4	89	54.2	64	40.0
Buchanan			1	.4			1	.8
Nader	8	10.3	9	4.9	12	7.2	3	2.0
Total	76	100.0	180	100.0	163	100.0	160	100.0

	Gender				Outside			
	Male		Female		Yes		No/NS	
	f	%	f	%	f	%	f	%
Gore	131	46.1	154	49.8	77	54.0	77	46.4
Bush	140	49.1	134	43.5	58	40.5	76	45.9
Buchanan			2	.6			2	1.1
Nader	14	4.8	19	6.1	8	5.6	11	6.6
Total	284	100.0	309	100.0	142	100.0	165	100.0

The impact of Nader could especially be seen in the key swing state of Florida, where he was heading toward 6 percent of the vote. Our poll revealed real strength in the Democratic bastion of Miami/South Florida, where we showed him getting 7 percent. I am a longtime fan of Ralph Nader and we have been close friends for decades. While it is clear that he did in fact have a negative impact on Gore's quest for the presidency, I do suppose we can still wonder how a sitting vice president did not win in a landslide following eight years of peace and prosperity.

There was in fact some confusion about the new ballot design in Florida. The perennial Socialist candidate David McReynolds scored more votes in Florida than he received in the rest of the forty-nine states combined, mainly because his name appeared where the vice-presidential candidate Joe Lieberman's should have been.[12] Conservative commentator Pat Buchanan similarly benefited from the ballot design. It was an optical illusion and probably cost Gore several thousand votes. It was also no small help to Bush that the governor of the state was his very popular younger brother Jeb. Governor Jeb Bush had appointed a political loyalist to the position of secretary of state, Katherine Harris, who ultimately ruled in Bush's favor.

But there was a crucial side note that we obtained from postelection polling. One of the most important and prescient questions I ever asked during my career in polling came by way of Alan Elsner, chief political correspondent for Reuters, right before Thanksgiving in 2000—three weeks after the election. Elsner asked me to go back into the field for Monday through Wednesday before Thanksgiving, and he had a unique and important question. To those who identified themselves as having voted for Gore, he wondered, if Bush were declared the winner, would they consider Bush the "legitimate" president of the United States? We would ask the same question about Gore to Bush voters.

Prior to this time, the legitimacy of an elected president had come up only a few times in American history. First, in 1824, Andrew Jackson lost a four-way race for president, which threw the election to the House of Representatives and gave us John Quincy Adams.[13] Jackson's people charged the Speaker of the House Henry Clay with corruption in manipulating the vote, especially fishy after Clay was "rewarded" with an appointment as secretary of state. (This "corrupt bargain" was later debunked.) Second, of course, was the Abraham Lincoln victory in 1860 in the northern states, which allowed him to win a majority of the electoral college and caused the southern states to secede.[14] Finally, there was the Compromise of 1877, which involved the House delegations of three southern states switching their votes to Rutherford B. Hayes in exchange for ending the US Army occupation of those states, even though Hayes had lost the popular vote.[15]

But here we were in 2000, and no one talked about secession or a hopeless deadlock between north and south or Democrats and Republicans. The results of our poll were stunning.[16] Among Gore supporters, 47 percent acknowledged that Bush would be the legitimately elected president, while 30 percent felt the election would be stolen. By contrast, among Bush voters, 60 percent told us that Gore would not be legitimate, while only 21 percent said he would be legitimate. Let's understand this result fully. Our findings did not merely suggest opposition or dislike; these voters were saying that they would not accept the results of the election. It was an actual challenge to our democracy.[17]

Table 1.3. Reuters/Zogby National Poll, November 22, 2000
MOE +/- 4.0 Percentage Points

Bush Voters

| | Total | | Region | | | | | | | |
| | | | East | | South | | CentGrLk | | West | |
	f	%	f	%	f	%	f	%	f	%
Legitimate	71	21.4	19	27.5	12	12.9	23	21.9	17	26.0
Stolen	200	60.1	31	44.6	66	71.6	65	61.2	38	58.8
NS	61	18.4	19	27.9	14	15.5	18	16.9	10	15.2
Total	333	100.0	69	100.0	92	100.0	107	100.0	65	100.0

(continued)

Table 1.3. Reuters/Zogby National Poll, November 22, 2000 MOE +/- 4.0 Percentage Points, *Continued*

	Party					
	Democrat		Republican		Independent	
	f	%	f	%	f	%
Legitimate	22	49.9	20	10.4	29	31.1
Stolen	15	34.6	140	71.6	45	48.0
NS	7	15.5	35	17.9	20	20.8
Total	44	100.0	196	100.0	94	100.0

	Age Group-B									
	18–24		25–34		35–54		55–69		70+	
	f	%	f	%	f	%	f	%	f	%
Legitimate	11	52.7	11	39.9	20	17.3	18	20.0	9	13.2
Stolen	7	34.0	15	55.1	76	64.3	54	61.2	45	64.5
NS	3	13.3	1	4.9	22	18.4	17	18.8	16	22.3
Total	21	100.0	28	100.0	118	100.0	89	100.0	70	100.0

	2000 Presidential Choice									
	Bush		Buchanan		Nader		Other		NV/NS	
	f	%	f	%	f	%	f	%	f	%
Legitimate	40	15.1	1	40.3	14	40.8	3	56.6	14	49.8
Stolen	184	69.7			10	29.0			6	22.9
NS	40	15.2	1	59.7	10	30.1	2	43.4	7	27.3
Total	265	100.0	2	100.0	33	100.0	6	100.0	27	100.0

Gore Voters

	Total		Region							
			East		South		CentGrLk		West	
	f	%	f	%	f	%	f	%	f	%
Legitimate	159	46.9	42	47.8	31	43.2	47	42.7	39	56.1
Stolen	101	29.9	27	30.6	29	40.0	30	27.7	15	21.9
NS	79	23.2	19	21.6	12	16.8	32	29.6	15	22.0
Total	339	100.0	89	100.0	72	100.0	109	100.0	69	100.0

	Party					
	Democrat		Republican		Independent	
	f	%	f	%	f	%
Legitimate	85	41.8	16	55.0	58	54.5
Stolen	75	36.6	3	10.8	24	22.0
NS	44	21.6	10	34.3	25	23.5
Total	204	100.0	28	100.0	107	100.0

	Age Group-B									
	18–24		25–34		35–54		55–69		70+	
	f	%	f	%	f	%	f	%	f	%
Legitimate	21	66.7	17	33.6	53	43.9	31	47.6	34	50.5
Stolen	9	27.8	21	41.4	41	34.4	14	21.8	15	21.9
NS	2	5.5	13	25.1	26	21.7	20	30.6	18	27.6
Total	31	100.0	51	100.0	120	100.0	65	100.0	67	100.0

	2000 Presidential Choice									
	Gore		Buchanan		Nader		Other		NV/NS	
	f	%	f	%	f	%	f	%	f	%
Legitimate	116	42.8	1	59.7	18	54.1	5	85.5	19	69.2
Stolen	89	32.7	1	40.3	8	23.7			4	14.3
NS	66	24.4			7	22.2	1	14.5	5	16.5
Total	271	100.0	2	100.0	33	100.0	6	100.0	27	100.0

Really, just one in five Bush voters told us that the Supreme Court victory would make Gore the legitimate president. This number included merely 10 percent of Republicans in our sample, 18 percent of voters over sixty-five, and 11 percent of born-again voters. While Gore supporters were more open to the legitimacy of a Bush "victory," the numbers were not particularly impressive. Not only would this situation mean no voter mandate for the next president, but it also offered an early peek into a troubled, hyperpartisan future.

By 2003, I would continue to examine this polarization with a poll outlining the demographics, behavior, and beliefs of two warring nations: red states (those states voting for Bush) versus blue states (those voting for Gore). Remember, some of these states had been designated their color by only a matter of a few thousand, or in the case of Florida, a few hundred votes. This was two full decades before Donald Trump's Big Lie, denying his loss in 2020, and the attack on Congress on January 6, 2021.[18]

In that late 2003 poll we were already able to see a significant division by more than politics and ideology. The country was being torn asunder demographically and culturally. Much more was at stake in the election of 2000 than the fate of two men or two opposition parties. As our polling after the 2000 election had revealed, we began to see a real challenge to the national community that James Madison and his colleagues worked so hard to put together over two hundred years earlier. Getting the election numbers right was always gratifying, but seeing the bigger picture—our future—unfold was capturing a much more powerful tornado in the making. Good polling did that. Election accuracy is the gravy on the mashed potatoes. But the mashed potatoes for dinner are what it is really all about.

Exhibit B: No Polling—
Flashback to Early November 1980

Major polls had led us to believe that the 1980 election was a close presidential race between incumbent Democrat Jimmy Carter and Republican challenger Ronald Reagan.[19] Carter presided over a country that was described as being in a "malaise" as a result of stagflation.[20] It had suffered another international humiliation as Iranian revolutionaries held hundreds of American embassy officials hostage.[21] But Reagan, having served as two-term governor of California, was viewed as dangerously ultraconservative, out of the mainstream ideologically, a threat to stability, and perhaps too old at sixty-nine to assume the presidential mantle. Add to the mix a moderate Republican congressman, John Anderson from Illinois, running as an independent, polling very well among moderates from both parties. Polls by the networks as well as the venerable independents like Gallup and Harris had the race neck and neck, with Anderson holding his own in the teens. Most Americans felt that the incumbent would win, as Reagan was simply too far out.[22]

By Election Day, reports suggested that Carter was in a funk and Reagan was upbeat. Somehow over the weekend Reagan picked up momentum. The man was transformed into a kindly grandfather and optimist, a force for positive change over the hapless Carter. Results were not even close: Reagan won the popular vote by ten points, 51 percent to 41 percent, as Anderson bottomed out at 7 percent.[23] Reagan won forty-four out of fifty states and walloped Carter with 489 electoral college votes, leaving Carter with only 49 of the 538 total. Reagan won among most groups who voted, especially redefining the senior vote and the "marriage gap"—that is, married voters (especially women) were much more likely to vote Republican than single women, a trend that would become even more pronounced over the next two decades.[24]

What happened? When did it transform and why? We are only left with speculation, because we have no real data leading up to Election Day itself. The last recorded polls were a week earlier, and no public polls were reported after Friday before the vote. I was a community activist in my home town of Utica, New York, not a pollster, at the time, and I recall speaking with two longtime Democratic Party stalwarts, both women, who told me as the polls were closing that they ended up voting for Reagan. It pained them, but as one put it, "I figured things couldn't possibly get worse, so it was time for a change." I have always used this interaction as my chief talking point about the 1980 outcome.[25] But it was not data. It was not Iowa or California or New Mexico polling or other bellwether election results. This was a case of no polling.

I have remained informed by the views I hear on a daily basis from voters in my community, and I feel that this improves my data. I also feel that the reverse is true—the data I collect from my polling rounds out and gives context to anecdotes heard along the way. But the polling industry made two important decisions following the 1980 debacle. First, don't release exit polls before the polling places are closed in a state. And second, conduct polling as late as possible to capture any last-minute trends. By 2000, new technologies also had enabled us to do polling more efficiently and more quickly.

The difference was simple over the twenty-year span: by 2000 we had tangible evidence of what happened late in the game and why. We were able to refine it down to specific voting groups and we, along with the CBS News pollsters, were the only ones to see it. We learned a valuable lesson: keep the lights on until the very end. Today, with as many as 10–14 percent (in my experience) of voters telling us that they make up their minds on Election Day, it is vital that we have a record to inform us about how and when decisions are made.[26] But I fear that polls are increasingly misunderstood. Sometimes there are just mistakes. Other times, they are misread and misrepresented by folks who really should know better. Still other times, only the most sensational result is reported and the important stuff is ignored. In recent years, polls have simply become the whipping boy of those who are angry at the results.

Since 2016, no sooner are votes being counted on election night than TV news people are ready to declare that the polls were wrong. However, for the most part, polls have done remarkably well. You have to know what polls can and are really supposed to do—and, more important, what they cannot always tell us. So, for starters, we must understand the limits of polling and have reasonable expectations for what they are saying. However, instead of dismissing polls that "miss" the final result by two whole percentage points, more time needs to be spent assessing what they are really telling us could happen and why.

This book offers some recent history and a guide to things I have learned (and done!) in a lifetime of poll taking and poll watching. First, I will try to demystify both the science and the art of polling—mainly, I hope, in lay terms. In a democracy, there is no need for (and there are too many pitfalls in serving up) mumbo jumbo. How do we draw samples? How do we ask questions? How do we really discover what people are truly thinking and what presses their buttons?

From there I will relate how some myths have arisen that try to explain what happened in key elections in recent history—mistakes that became legendary misinterpretations. I will also offer counterinterpretations based on the actual polling I was doing at the time. I will take a critical look at the faux industries that polling has spawned—aggregating averages and making daily (hourly) betting odds by mixing different polls into one cauldron and pretending that a mystical data science has been created. The industries involving aggregation of polling numbers are noble, but how they are used and interpreted and represented is an atrocity.

Having now polled in 195 countries and having among the best results in very difficult situations like elections in Mexico, Iran, democratically inexperienced and ill-prepared Albania, supercharged Israel, anti-American (at least anti–American pollsters) Canada, and revolutionary Tunisia, I will explain the dangers of doing good polling beyond the United States, how to apply rules learned domestically to culturally sensitive regions and people, and why we got things right.

My goal is to present a very public look at how strategists, campaign managers, fundraisers, and candidates look (or at least need to look) at polls. We'll see how they know the right questions to ask, and draw the samples that most closely approximate what the demographics of the final turnout look like, and ultimately how the public and those who would "interpret" for the public should be reading polls.

Lessons from Chapter 1

Leave the lights on longer. Just like the early bird that catches the worm, the very last poll closest to the election has at least a better chance of catching the last-minute change or trend line. It has always amazed me how few postmortems are done after campaigns, and I mean among both winning and losing teams. Most campaigns in the United States are on the local level, and there simply are not exit polls to comb through. Budgets are usually too small to accommodate last-minute polling, especially since the results of polls taken up to the day of the election will not assist in changing strategy or tweaking media ads. But final tracking can yield important information for both sides: When did undecided voters break one way? What factors drove their decisions? Is there anything that could have been done to change their minds? Which demographics and other subgroups were pivotal? This is important information for both the short term and long-term strategies in the future. On the state and national levels, there should be no black holes. The 1980 election has only speculation about why it turned out the way it did, and that does not serve historians well.

In 2000, I was polling for Reuters and NBC News. Longtime GOP pollsters Public Opinion Strategies were polling for the Bush campaign. Why was I so right and they so wrong? On my end, I applied weights to all the demographics that needed them, and my results were very close to what the exit polls would show. What happened with the other polling group? They are among the best in the business. Were they just posturing to bolster their candidate and intimidate the other side—and me?

The important takeaway from these pages is that polls play an important role in the lives of those of us who live in democracies. First, they help connect us to each other. Are my views on certain issues consistent with a majority, or am I on the fringes? Does my candidate have a chance to win? And if so, what does he or she have to do? Should I make a last-minute financial contribution, or is it wasted? Who are we as a people? And how intense are we—as a whole and as smaller groups—on key issues? I have seen for decades how polls can be misinterpreted, how they can be twisted to fit preassumptions, and how they can destroy candidates. Even worse, I have seen how they can be abused to portray an America that doesn't exist.

Sadly, there are many examples of bad polling driving bad decisions, and at times I had a front-row seat to these abuses and wrongheaded interpretations. In the following pages, I lay out for scholars, political professionals, business decision-makers, students, and political junkies the key elements of this misunderstood (and at times mishandled) industry. My hope is that you find it illuminating and useful as a guide to understanding a vital service in a democracy. I want readers to feel empowered to read the information better and learn to judge what is useful and what is misleading as we head to the election of 2024—another in a series of "*the* most important elections in our lifetime."[27]

CHAPTER 2

A Brief Primer on Polling
HOW TO DESIGN A GOOD SAMPLE AND ASK THE RIGHT QUESTIONS

The following is a recent and absolutely true story. I was having a colonoscopy, and the physician recognized my surname.

I was in a compromised position, and he said to me, "How do you get people to answer their phones?"

"Well, not like this."

I have had to endure similar polling-related questions while on the treadmill during a nuclear stress test, at Little League games, and in the reception line at a wake. Though I am an erstwhile Catholic, this is one of the reasons I haven't been to confession in decades! The answer to the physician's question, however, revolves around the social changes brought on by new technologies. To avoid misconceptions and preconceptions, here is what we pollsters do and how we do it.

First off, some basics. It used to be so simple. When I started my business in September 1984, 93 percent of US households had a landline.[1] Socially and culturally, a phone call was still a big deal. Very few Americans had an answering machine, and it was not uncommon to hear a respondent shush others at home by saying, "Please be quiet, someone is calling me from New York and asking me important questions." Back then, polling response rates averaged 65 percent, and refusals were generally polite. Sampling was done by a process called random-digit dialing, which meant essentially, given the aim of random probability, every household had to have the same chance of being selected as any other. To ensure that unlisted phone numbers were represented in the sample pool, area codes and exchanges (i.e., the next three numbers) were drawn per region, and then the last four digits were scrambled. With huge response rates, pollsters could afford both the time and the cost of dialing lots of nonexistent phone numbers. For my part, my early tests showed that I could obtain pretty much the same (and similarly accurate) results using listed telephone numbers, as I explained in detail in the political campaign consultants' bible, *Campaigns and Elections*, in which I wrote a column for years.[2]

Then technology, and with it some broad changes in our culture, intervened. First, there were answering machines, and then answering services. Citizens could subscribe to a service known as *69, which allowed them to call us back immediately to check on our validity. Picture us in those early days with only twenty-four phones, and people hanging up and calling us back immediately. It was a nightmare. Then came cell phones, then email, and so on. People, myself included, were empowered and enabled to simply not answer phone calls anymore. Telemarketing and prank calls muddied the waters, and spam calls are more often the ones the public receives. Response rates plummeted and now can represent as low as 2–3 percent of actual dials in major urban areas.[3]

I recall how often I would engage some of our interviewers as they were leaving six-hour shifts in our call center, and discover that they spent their days talking to only one or two people. Some became so discouraged that they stopped working for us. That problem was compounded whenever we used random-digit dialing because of the additional burden of dialing so many nonworking numbers. Further, millions of Americans have been empowered by the Do Not Call Registry, allowing states' attorneys general to issue cease-and-desist orders to pollsters. Technically, market research and polling companies are exempt from these laws, but when we are on tight deadlines and people are threatening to sue, who needs the battle?

We, along with the famed Harris Poll, were the first to develop our own nationwide lists of emails and build panels to do some political online polling using randomly drawn probability samples.[4] We advertised on other political and consumer websites, purchased email addresses by the hundreds of thousands, and asked our telephone poll respondents whether they would like to be on an online poll panel. Once we had collected several hundred thousand clean and verified panel members, we tested the panels with polling. It involved the same overall principles as drawing telephone samples: we broke the panel into regions and drew a random sample of the amount we needed, and then we sent invitations. From the beginning we built in mechanisms so that invitees could not forward the survey to others, take the survey twice, or use any other ways of gaming it.

We of course continued to grow the sample pool until 2008, when we decided to go to major list brokers and purchase one-time-use panels. We continued to the greatest degree possible to abide by the rules of random probability sampling—everyone in the total pool had the same chance of being selected as everyone else. Online political polling proved to be challenging for us at first, but by 2008 we were very comfortable with it. Nationwide samples would have a 15–20 percent response rate, which was much better than either listed phone numbers or random-digit-dialed numbers. We have found that online polling yields not only better response rates but also better distributed samples and more accurate representations of Blacks, Latinos, young people, and lower-income respondents.

Today, pollsters have multiple methods available to use. Much rarer is the exclusive, one-size-fits-all landline telephone methodology. Some polls still require the spontaneous and anonymous response of the live telephone call. Perhaps the subject matter is too sensitive, the contact needs to be more personal, or the universe (a small town, a group of airline pilots, employees of hair salons) is insufficient in size for drawing an online panel. In addition to lower response rates, this method of live calling is complicated by the need to make a large percentage of calls to cell phones, in which the response rates are dismal. Many polls involve so much more than simply asking who the respondent intends to vote for. Typically, a poll can be forty to fifty questions, and calling a cell phone is a nuisance, annoying, and wastes the respondent's minutes if they have a telephone plan.

Live calls are also expensive, and not every client has a budget for that. On the other end of the spectrum are interactive voice response (IVR) polls, more commonly called robocalls. These can be done cheaply, and for the most part efficiently. Among the drawbacks are that cell phones cannot be dialed—robocalls to cell phones are prohibited by law in all fifty states. With so many people using only cell phones, this process limits the accuracy of the polling.

Online polling is now my preferred technology because 92–93 percent of households in the United States (and a higher percentage of likely voters) use the internet, and thus have access to email and are facile enough with usage that they can respond to surveys.[5] The number of adults with internet access in the United States grew by 8.4 million just from 2021 to 2022, so we are still in a very dynamic situation.[6] Panel members can answer questions on their own time; complete part of the survey, stop, and then return; and do not have to feel uncomfortable talking to any strangers. This latter factor alone accounts for more honesty on hot-button issues.[7]

In the past decade we have begun to use a form of hybrid methodology, which involves, as the term suggests, a combination of any of the above—some live calls, some online, and some text messages inviting respondents to a secure website to take the survey. We have had to get creative and respond to a world where technology has demanded change, just like almost every other industry.

For the most part, growing numbers of people are simply too busy to talk on the telephone. Others, particularly teens and twentysomethings, never answer their phones. Parents, try calling your kids on the phone, and let me know how it goes. The telephone had been the primary means of communication for families, friends, and businesspeople for decades. Then, by the 1980s, as more Americans were working, families broke down, children became engaged in many activities outside the home, fathers and mothers needed to take on extra jobs, and telemarketers invaded our private time, the telephone became more a tool of choice than necessity. We could now technologically and socially choose which calls to take and which to ignore. The simple answer to the doctor's question that opens this chapter was that we could not get people to or make people answer the phone. Response rates plummeted. We were also competing with fake polls that tried to lure people into supporting candidates or entering scams.

On the phones, we would first have to get people to agree to take the poll. Our interviewers were instructed to say it was "only a brief poll" because, first, no one would bother to take a "long" one. Second, I suppose if we consider there have been forty-five thousand years of human existence and average life expectancy for humans is today about seventy-nine years, fifteen to twenty-five minutes is really pretty brief. For political polls, we then would have to screen to ensure they were registered to vote and that they were at least likely to vote. We needed them to identify their party (or nonparty) affiliation, and would lose more people by then. This was less cumbersome in the days when people just simply answered their landlines.

Today's options are more encouraging. We continue to use existing (and constantly validated and updated) panels of people who have agreed to take surveys. With fifteen-million-plus and growing pools of voters who are demographically representative of the adult US population in this panel, we are then capable of drawing a random probability sample by region and by sending invitations. We have found over the years that few people get to take more than a handful of surveys per year, most of them just one.

In politics we have to screen for likely voters.[8] We need to be wary of political polls that report only a sample of just "adults" or "registered voters." There is a difference in the demographics and sensibilities of each group, and it should be understood that in matters of politics and policy, voters really count. Even if it is months before an election, we still need to sift out "likely voters," because ultimately it is their votes that count, and also because we need to be able to compare apples with apples to show how likely voters have shifted or stayed the same over the campaign.

We also need to ensure that the sample is well distributed. Generally, but not always, raw samples, regardless of phone or internet methodology, yield results that underrepresent younger voters—these days many of whom are people of color (nonwhites) and people from lower-income households.[9] In every instance, some form of weighting needs to be done in order to be representative of voter turnout. I have often said that in addition to asking skilled questions, factoring sample weights is a part of the "art" of polling. Ultimately, we pollsters need to produce a sample that reflects the projected turnout model. This task is not easy, and it is especially difficult the closer we get to the actual election.

There are indeed likely voters who have not made up their minds yet about voting, plus those who are fungible in their candidate choice. In many instances they have just started to pay attention to the campaign, are new voters, or consider themselves unaffiliated with any party. This situation leaves us little to go on from their profiles as to which way they will turn. We use exit polls in previous similar elections as a benchmark, but we always need to be mindful that demographic and attitudinal changes might very well have occurred since the most recent election. Is there any reason that fewer Black or Hispanic voters will go to the polls? Will more or fewer young people opt to sit this new election out? Are younger women more or less energized? Is there an issue or candidate that mobilizes one group of voters or particularly alienates another group? Is there any reason to think that there are changes in party affiliation or ideological thinking in the past few years? These are important variables, and any (or all) could be decisive in the outcome.

For decades I have advised students who have expressed an interest in a career in polling that it is by no means enough to just be good in statistics. As I wrote in my 2016 book, *We Are Many, We Are One: Neo-Tribes and Tribal Analytics in 21st Century America*, a good pollster "requires the sensibility of the artist, the ability to understand people of the social scientist, and interpretive skills of the novelist, philosopher and poet."[10] Thus, I have always recommended loading up on social sciences and the humanities, reading novels, and volunteering for campaigns (not as strategist or communications director, but as someone who hands out leaflets in the rain and knocks on doors). Polling is very much a right-brain activity, too.

Good polls go well beyond the horse race. Barometric readings are important, like whether the country is headed in the right or wrong direction; whether folks feel that their personal or household finances are better off, worse off, or about the same as they were four years ago; whether an incumbent deserves to be reelected or it is time for someone new; and the top issues, including scales to determine intensity levels. I have found the need to be constantly flexible in the kinds of questions I ask to draw people out, to obtain a stronger sense of who they really are and what drives their decisions and behaviors. Simple questions like "Generally speaking, would you say that things in the country are headed in the right direction, or are they off on the wrong track?" used to provide a clear reading on the mood of voters overall and by subgroup. It was simple and straightforward. But in the past twenty years it has become pretty useless, at least in the United States. Given the levels of intense partisanship, results on this question yield mainly a partisan response.[11] If the incumbent president is Democrat, Democrats will tend to feel things are going in the right direction and the opposition Republicans will overwhelmingly give a thumbs-down. The reverse is also true. Even if more Democrats jump ship on their president, they still have to consider whether they would cast their vote for the other party, which has moved far to the ideological extreme or has taken a position (e.g., abortion, election denial) that they cannot possibly support. In short, good pollsters need to be constantly vigilant in finding new ways to discover what really moves voters to act.

One disagreement among political pollsters is the value placed on party identification. For many in what I would call the "establishment" of the industry (i.e., Gallup, Pew Research, the television network/national newspaper combinations), "party ID" has been seen as a "trailer variable," meaning that it is more fungible depending on external factors like the economy, quality of the candidates, or a single hot issue. Thus, if a voter has leaned Republican over the years, he or she may be currently put off by the overall atmosphere, fear of losing a job, the performance of a GOP incumbent, and so on, and thus lean toward the Democratic candidate.[12] In this view, the respondent could possibly change their identification to Democrat. I have always been more inclined to see party identification as a "lead variable," meaning that it is normally as solid as a demographic in telling us who and what a respondent represents. Thus, even though a respondent may favor a candidate who is the opposite of the party they normally select, they still are more than likely to identify with their original party, screen their information from that long-held point of view, and still vote for their party's preferences under regular circumstances.

Because of my take on this, I include a weight for party identification if I see the results of my raw sample overrepresenting or underrepresenting unfairly. With that said, as I will discuss a little later, I have never had to dramatically apply weights for party identification. I have been truly puzzled by some pollsters who report wide swings in party identification. I have seen in election campaigns some prominent polls with samples including as many as 42 percent Democrats and as low as 24 percent Republicans. I can report that my raw, unweighted samples normally result in party identifications that are at most within a few points of the final outcome. And they are mainly even closer to where they should be once I have applied all other weights (like age, gender, and race). I prefer my method because, while it recognizes that there can be changes in who shows up to vote, my samples are generally more stable in the party and demographic models used.

Although party identification is an attitude and not a fixed characteristic, political scientists have long recognized that it is a very stable attitude. Gradual shifts in the balance of party loyalties in the electorate are not unusual—Republicans have gained ground in relation to Democrats in recent years, for example. However, dramatic changes over a short period of time are quite rare.[13]

Asking the right questions is equally vital to yielding accurate results. I make a lot of use of values-based questions. Instead of relying on ones that are

so boring and neutered as to reveal nothing about the hearts and souls of voters, I prefer policy questions linked to actual values, so that I am learning more about what drives choices that voters make. I also need to learn more about the intensity of their feelings, because how strongly a minority feels about an issue can be much more useful to me than what the majority feels.

There are ways to plumb the depths of people's feelings and get a whole lot more information about them than simple one-dimensional questions. Instead of the basic "agree/disagree" or "support/oppose" paradigm about issues and policies they know nothing about, consider the following pairings:

> Example 1: Do you support or oppose legislation that would prohibit economic development on land near XYZ Lake?

> vs.

> There is a proposed law that supporters claim will protect endangered species that are vital to the ecosystem and will ensure that XYZ Lake will stay pristine. Opponents argue that this proposed law is another example of government overreach and that preventing further economic development will mean no new jobs. Which comes closer to your own view?

Please note that within the second question we allow both sides a fair and symmetrical expression of their position. Also note that the opposing statements do not have to be dichotomous. What really is going on here is that the second set provides balanced information, and each side gets to present the values of its case: preservation, clean water, the environment versus less government encroachment and fewer jobs.

> Example 2: When it comes to abortion, do you describe yourself as more pro-choice or more pro-life?

> vs.

> Which of the following best describes your position on abortion?
> Terminating a fetus is tantamount to manslaughter and should be treated that way in a court of law.
> Matters related to pregnancy should involve a woman and her physician. It is a private matter and should be protected.

Again, this is not presented as a matter of opposites—just a fair representation of both sides. I have discovered over the years that many people are conflicted about this issue and believe both sides equally. But we need to find out which argument draws out their sensibility more.

Example 3: Do you agree or disagree that former baseball star Pete Rose should be inducted into the Baseball Hall of Fame?

vs.

Supporters of Pete Rose say that he had more hits than any player in Major League Baseball history, three World Series championships, was a seventeen-time All-Star, and possessed a winning attitude that was an inspiration. If moral behavior were relevant, then players like Ty Cobb, Babe Ruth, and Mickey Mantle, to name only a few, would never be enshrined. Opponents argue that Pete Rose violated not only professional sports ethics but also the law by betting on his own team and that the baseball commissioner who issued the lifetime ban had to establish a benchmark to discourage such behavior in the future.

This is, of course, not a public policy matter, but the values focus is very revealing because we will obtain a sense of how important it is to people and which is more important, sports accomplishment or ethics.

My 2016 book on "neo-tribes" and "tribal analytics" gives us new ways to think about how people identify themselves.[14] Our new typology involved extensive survey work with open-ended questions, allowing people to define their beliefs, values, priorities, self-descriptions, life experiences, and rules governing their lives. Ours was a bottom-up approach that led to the packaging of what can be called "cognitive demographics" or "neo-tribes." We found in separate studies that identification in any of these neo-tribes was more predictive in situations and voting than race, age, or ethnicity. We also found significant overlap between differing neo-tribes, what we called "tribal border crossings," whereby there could be room for exploiting commonalities between, say, members of the "Happy Hedonists" and the "God Squad" on issues or in predictive behavior.

It is this kind of thinking and the use of data as validation that establishes a good pollster from simply a numbers cruncher. There is a difference.

Reading Crosstabs—I Mean, *Really* Reading Crosstabs

Here is an inside look at polls that I did for a conservative group founded by Ronald Reagan's associates, the Committee for Democracy. Several states have initiatives to pass state legislation and push Congress to support clean water by placing limits on private businesses located near rivers and streams. We asked voters in five states similar questions, adjusted for each local river protection. Here are just two questions from one state, Oregon, that will demonstrate how I read a poll.

Table 2.1.   John Zogby Strategies Survey of Oregon Likely Voters, December 16–17, 2020
N=403 Margin of Error +/– 5 Percentage Points

Q: Would you favor a proposal to add protections to rivers across Oregon being voted on by Congress in a new law or simply being implemented by the president through an executive order?

	Party							
	Total		Democrat		Republican		Independent	
	f	%	f	%	f	%	f	%
Voted by Congress	231	57.4	79	55.7	64	66.2	89	53.8
Imposed by President	93	23.0	41	29.0	18	18.4	34	20.5
Not Sure	79	19.6	22	15.3	15	15.4	42	25.7
Total	403	100.0	141	100.0	97	100.0	165	100.0

	Age Group									
	Total		18–29		30–49		50–64		65+	
	f	%	f	%	f	%	f	%	f	%
Voted by Congress	231	57.4	38	56.1	67	50.4	68	65.2	58	59.5
Imposed by President	93	23.0	13	19.1	41	30.8	21	19.6	18	18.7
Not Sure	79	196	17	24.8	25	18.8	16	15.2	21	21.8
Total	403	100.0	69	100.0	133	100.0	105	100.0	97	100.0

Q: Which of the following statements comes closer to your view? Statement A: When new environmental protections are added to wild and scenic rivers in Oregon, rural communities can benefit economically because traditional jobs in ranching and farming can coexist alongside new jobs created from recreation and tourism. Statement B: When new environmental protections are added to wild and scenic rivers in Oregon, rural communities are hurt economically because traditional jobs in ranching and farming cannot coexist alongside new jobs created from recreation and tourism.

	Any College?				Race			
	College		No College		White		Not White	
	f	%	f	%	f	%	f	%
Can co-exist	164	70.7	113	66.4	229	67.5	48	79.8
Cannot co-exist	28	11.9	23	13.7	42	12.4	6	10.5
Not Sure	40	17.4	34	19.9	68	20.0	6	9.8
Total	233	100.0	170	100.0	339	100.0	60	100.0

(continued)

Table 2.1. John Zogby Strategies Survey of Oregon Likely Voters, *Continued*

Q: Which of the following statements comes closer to your view? Statement A: When new environmental protections are added to wild and scenic rivers in Oregon, rural communities can benefit economically because traditional jobs in ranching and farming can coexist alongside new jobs created from recreation and tourism. Statement B: When new environmental protections are added to wild and scenic rivers in Oregon, rural communities are hurt economically because traditional jobs in ranching and farming cannot coexist alongside new jobs created from recreation and tourism.

	Gender					
	Total		Male		Female	
	f	%	f	%	f	%
Can co-exist	277	68.8	146	72.5	131	65.1
Cannot co-exist	51	12.6	24	12.0	27	13.3
Not Sure	75	18.6	31	15.5	44	21.6
Total	403	100.0	201	100.0	202	100.0

	Live							
	Large City		Small City		Suburbs		Rural Area	
	f	%	f	%	f	%	f	%
Can co-exist	86	75.6	48	69.8	83	69.1	60	60.0
Cannot co-exist	6	5.2	9	13.3	15	12.4	21	20.9
Not Sure	22	19.2	12	16.9	22	18.5	19	19.1
Total	114	100.0	69	100.0	120	100.0	101	100.0

	Ideology											
	V Liberal		Liberal		Moderate		Conservative		V Conservative		Libertarian	
	f	%	f	%	f	%	f	%	f	%	f	%
Can co-exist	50	97.9	78	83.0	74	61.8	43	52.5	15	41.9	8	93.3
Cannot co-exist			4	4.3	19	16.2	15	18.0	10	29.2		
Not Sure	1	2.1	12	12.7	26	22.0	24	29.5	10	28.9	1	6.7
Total	51	100.0	94	100.0	120	100.0	81	100.0	36	100.0	8	100.0

| | Hunter? | | | | | | Fisherman? | | | |
| | Total | | Yes | | No | | Yes | | No | |
	f	%	f	%	f	%	f	%	f	%
Can co-exist	277	68.8	46	67.5	231	69.0	76	66.1	201	69.9
Cannot co-exist	51	12.6	10	14.2	41	12.3	18	15.3	33	11.6
Not Sure	75	18.6	12	18.3	62	18.6	21	18.6	53	18.5
Total	403	100.0	68	100.0	335	100.0	115	100.0	288	100.0

| | Water recreation enthusiast? | | | | Gun Owner | | | | | |
| | Yes | | No | | Current | | Former | | Never | |
	f	%	f	%	f	%	f	%	f	%
Can co-exist	124	69.2	153	68.5	71	66.0	27	66.9	166	73.4
Cannot co-exist	22	12.1	29	13.0	17	15.5	9	21.7	16	7.2
Not Sure	34	18.7	41	18.5	20	18.6	5	11.3	44	19.4
Total	180	100.0	223	100.0	108	100.0	40	100.0	226	100.0

If we simply accept conventional wisdom and history, Democrats and liberals mainly support strong federal intervention on matters related to preserving the environment and placing limits on economic development schemes that could harm rivers and streams. At the same time, Republicans and conservatives oppose efforts to obstruct investment and free-market decisions, especially if they hinder job creation. The polls we did in Oregon and the other states reveal a much more nuanced approach to these issues, one that can be exploited for political gain by both parties and provide a legislative win for solid majorities on all sides. First of all, there is strong support for congressional intervention on behalf of saving the rivers and streams from excessive private-sector development. In addition to huge support among Democrats and liberals, a majority of Republicans and conservatives, as well as moderates and independents, are actually in favor of federal intervention. Where we see the nuance is when we consider voters as more than just their partisan and ideological buckets. Thus we see our voters as hunters, anglers, hikers, and outdoors enthusiasts—identities and behaviors that are without partisan borders.

Our analysis to our client strongly urged them to present the results in these terms—things that congressional staff and representatives could identify with themselves. This is how we use polls. This example, just one of many, illustrates how polling can do more than find what separates us in the interest of discovering commonalities that can bridge gaps.

Lessons from Chapter 2

This one brief lesson from Oregon and other states is also a reminder to both the producers and the consumers of polls that this profession is not a one-dimensional, one-size-fits-all practice. Public pollsters need the clearest data to forecast elections or determine how best to cover campaigns. Private pollsters require this data quality to plot strategies and optimize resources to win campaigns. Scholars need accuracy to study how humans behave and to develop public policies. And clients need to know how to build, develop, market, and measure employee and consumer satisfaction, and much more. Discussions of methodology can be enlightening, but I fear they turn too often into which method is the best for fitting the greatest number of "nonresponse biases" on the head of a pin. That does not serve the field or humanity very well. Professional organizations like American Association for Public Opinion Research (AAPOR) form committees to respond to questions that cannot be answered satisfactorily. Their reports following the elections of 2016 and 2020 were filled with "probably," "cannot say with certainty," and "no real evidence of." No survey can ever be perfect, because we are dealing with flawed humans and all kinds of sources of mathematical errors. We can only strive for greatness. As Barack Obama (echoing Aristotle and Voltaire, among others) would have said, "Don't let the perfect be the enemy of the good."

Polling is indeed a science, but we are in a world where many old rules no longer apply. How do we claim that "every household in the country has the same chance of being selected as any other" when so many households take themselves out of the game before we even get started, refuse to answer the phone when it rings, relegate invitations for online polls to the spam folder, or are unwilling to be bothered on their cell phones? When response rates are 2–3 percent, is that truly "probability" sampling? As in every other industry, we have had to be innovative. Don't be afraid to try new methods. And never be afraid to riff, to speculate, to find patterns. Don't be fearful of going places that others are too timid to explore.

At the same time, don't ever forget we pollsters poll people, not numbers. Behind every response is a real human being who laughs and cries (if they even have time to do that!). They are busy keeping a job, getting the kids to school on time, worrying about the mortgage or promotion, running three different ways to soccer practice, violin, or family court. Try to capture their attention with questions that reveal what matters to them, that pique their interest, that ask them about things they know and feel, and that get at who they really are instead of how neatly we can package them into our own preconceived boxes.

Know beforehand what you need to get out of the poll. Sure, you will need to get a straight up or down vote in a horse race or their approval or disapproval of an image. And you will have to scrutinize the crosstabs to see what the trend lines are among those you thought would support or oppose your client. But you are in the business of asking the "why" questions, so be able to have a robust series of questions about issues and messages and images to bolster whatever you find. And never be afraid of the counterintuitive or "black swan" answers. Public opinion is not a simple set of data points. It reveals personal stories, previous biases, connections to other people, loyalty, disappointment, surprises. Look at the answers that you did not expect to find and try to explain them.

CHAPTER 3

Getting the Polls Right and How to Read Them Right

The Zogby Poll became a household brand in 1994 when I declared to my media clients, the *New York Post* and Fox 5 television in New York City, that then State Senator George Pataki would probably defeat incumbent Governor Mario Cuomo in the gubernatorial race. Every other poll had Cuomo leading by 3–5 percentage points, and it was hard for pundits who live in one of the most politically insular villages in the United States, the Big Apple, to fathom that a national icon and the man who gave an amazing speech at the Democratic National Convention in 1984 (same folks!) could possibly lose an election in his own state. After that spellbinding speech that engaged his Italian background and framed the nation as a family, including the duty of the stronger members to ensure the well-being of the weaker, they saw him as a future president.[1] Cuomo could be captivating as a speaker, but he was also known to be darker and more brooding than former President Richard Nixon. Both of them had kept a list of enemies. Although he served three terms, when the longtime Democratic minority leader of the New York State Senate was asked what Cuomo's greatest accomplishment was, he said, "That speech," which I roughly translate as "words rather than deeds."

Although my poll was getting fairly well known in New York, and Cuomo was briefed every day on my results, when a reporter from Gannett News Service asked him whether he had seen "the latest Zogby poll," he responded, "I don't know who [John Zogby] is."[2] My polls had been on the front page of the *New York Post* for many weeks, but his dismissal, in a strange way, actually helped more in my becoming a household name. Later, pollster and Cuomo spokesman Joel Benenson told me that he said to the press, "We're not concerned about polls by every Tom, Dick, and Zogby who comes along."[3]

And, to be fair, I had Cuomo with a slight lead going into the election. But Pataki had been closing in daily, picking up undecided voters in the Republican strongholds of upstate New York. Even more important, with only hours to go before the polls opened, almost one in five Black voters in New York State were still "undecided" on who to vote for.[4] Cuomo suffered from a lower than normal voter turnout in Black precincts and lost. I picked up a clear trend line toward the challenger Pataki and away from Cuomo.

Exhibit C: Bad Polling Can Unfairly Hurt a Candidate

I have often been asked whether polling can impact the outcome of an election. I'm reluctant to concede that point, simply because there are so many examples of voters declaring their independence from the conventional wisdom and making their own choices. But for me there is one major example of polls that hurt a candidate. The 1996 presidential election is a case in which bad polling drove election coverage in a biased way and ultimately destroyed the presidential candidacy of Senator Bob Dole, Republican Senate majority leader and World War II hero. Dole had to endure the bias of pundits who compiled inaccurate polls. Throughout the 1996 campaign, he was forced to defend against media who labeled him a doomed nominee.[5] I was polling for Reuters in the 1996 campaign, and while I never really saw a tight race, my polls revealed at least a much more competitive one than the results of other colleagues. One particular October day, as Dole was campaigning in Columbus, Ohio, longtime ABC News White House correspondent Sam Donaldson introduced coverage of Dole's appearance as being twenty points behind President Clinton. At that point, he was really behind by seven points—a victory not quite within his grasp, but certainly not enough of a deficit to knock the wind out of his sails.

This was the election in which the Zogby Poll, daily tracking the national election for Reuters, became a global brand. In short, my final published result showed President Bill Clinton with 49 percent, Dole with 41 percent, and billionaire independent Ross Perot with 8 percent.[6] These were the exact results of the popular vote in the election. Polls by the major television networks and their daily newspaper partners had consistently showed Clinton leading by double digits over Dole, and their final published results ranged from ABC News/*Washington Post*'s twelve-point margin, through *USA Today*/Gallup's seventeen-point lead and CBS News/*New York Times*'s eighteen-point blowout.[7] I was on the lead panel at the annual AAPOR conference the following spring and sat with Everett Carll Ladd, the executive director of the Roper Center in Connecticut; Frank Newport, managing editor at Gallup; and Kathleen Frankovic, director of polling at CBS News.[8] Ladd caused quite a stir in the polling community with an op-ed in the *Wall Street Journal*, in which he said, "It is likely that pollsters and reporters dampened voters' interest, and hence participation, by announcing that the presidential contest was really no contest at all."[9] Frankovic, a brilliant researcher and very nice person, went through the tortuous process of explaining how she had done everything right—except that she had gotten the election so terribly wrong. That happens, but she made a great recovery by joining me four years later in seeing an Al Gore victory in the popular vote.

Is Party Identification a Lead Variable, or a Trailer Variable?

I took the opportunity to plow into my colleagues' daily tracking polls and final results in 1996, and I found where they made their mistakes. In each instance, they were oversampling Democrats and underrepresenting Republicans. I had learned early (in the 1980s and long before Donald Trump's MAGA phenomenon) that Republicans were less likely to answer polls.[10] Some of it was demographic—that is, a Democratic, blue-collar union household was more receptive to simply answering a call than the household of a Republican suburban physician. Some of it was also the early stages of a revolt against a longtime "Democratic elite," the desire to keep one's choice private. By the 1990s, conservative radio talk show hosts would actively encourage their followers to play mischief with the polls—even though they would cite the results religiously, especially the results that mirrored their own views.

Whatever the cause, I took the position that political party identification was a demographic characteristic—mainly inherited from parents—and hence in need of weighting to ensure that the parties' voters were represented as closely to their turnout in previous elections, as revealed in exit polls. Now that did not mean that party identification was immutable, just as at times there could be variations in the percentages of women or younger voters or voters of color. It only meant that there should be an extra effort to ensure sufficient and equitable representation. I admit this involves some artwork, and this helped launch a debate about party weighting among professional pollsters.[11] I engaged the debate as part of that highly contentious panel in 1997 I mentioned above.[12]

But what troubled me was that in 1996 I operated with an understanding that the party breakdown in my national samples should be 39 percent Democrats, 35 percent Republicans, and 26 percent independents. I based that solely on the 1992 presidential election exit polls. When my daily raw numbers (before weighting) came in, I never had to do more than a two- or three-point weight for party identification. Some of my colleagues would show samples of only 28 percent Republicans and 42 percent Democrats. No wonder they were off on their elections. We might want to dismiss this result as simply inaccurate polling, but, as noted above in the case of Bob Dole's visit to Columbus, Ohio, the results could be very damaging and were actually used to dictate how much and what kind of coverage a candidate received.

Exhibit D: Right versus Wrong in New Jersey

Something oddly troubling happened in the 1996 New Jersey Senate election between two congressmen, Democrat Bob Torricelli and Republican Dick Zimmer. The candidates started beating each other's brains out in March, so by October many voters had little use for either. I was polling this race for the *New York Post*, and what I noted with special interest was that one in five Black voters were still undecided when I started my daily tracking ten days before Election Day. The two candidates were neck and neck, but both in the low forties in terms of support. They would stay that way until the Thursday before the election. Torricelli would pull ahead, and it was because Black undecided voters were starting to break in his favor. By Saturday afternoon, he was in a ten-point lead over Zimmer.[13]

Humorously, the *New York Post* headline on Sunday before the election featured how polls were showing a Zimmer lead. And several prominent New Jersey pollsters did. The *Post* had endorsed Zimmer and was going to mold the story and headline to fit the needs of the editorial board. The one sentence that ended the story said simply, "In one other poll by Zogby International, commissioned by the *Post*, Torricelli led by 10 points." They paid for the poll, but they had to protect their editorial board's endorsement. Torricelli won 52.7 percent to 42.6 percent—a solid ten points!

But what was going on in New Jersey was a longer story. For years, the leading polling outfit in the Garden State had been the Eagleton Institute at Rutgers University. They had already had a decade of blowing New Jersey statewide races. In 1990, Eagleton showed incumbent US Senator Bill Bradley headed toward a seventeen-point victory over newcomer (and later Governor) Christine Todd Whitman. Despite the unpopularity of the Democratic Governor James Florio and the immense popularity of Republican President George H. W. Bush (three months before Operation Desert Storm), as well as the growing rage over a statewide tax increase pushed by Florio, the state's most prominent pollster saw an easy victory for the incumbent Democrat's Senate reelection. But election results showed the GOP challenger coming within 2 points of Bradley.[14]

Commentators were hard pressed to explain how Whitman came from behind without even considering that the race had actually been close for a while and the Eagleton outfit just missed the boat. The same held true in 1993 when

Whitman came back from an Eagleton Poll deficit to defeat incumbent Governor Florio. Despite Florio's unpopularity, no poll showed a Republican beating a Democrat. Again, Eagleton had Florio the Democrat ahead 48 percent to 39 percent in its final preelection poll.[15] To be fair, the university institute did report that Florio's support had declined from 52 percent to 48 percent from a poll two weeks earlier and that the numbers of undecided voters had grown from 8 percent to 13 percent. Nonetheless, its final poll before the election still suggested an electoral landslide. What made Whitman such a great closer? Polls, including the Eagleton Institute, still showed Florio headed to a victory. Once actual votes were counted, Florio had indeed held on to his 48 percent, but Whitman gained 9 percent to reach 49 percent and won the election The polls would miss it once more, but the media would again prefer to rely on misguided polling than upset their presumptions. Fact is that Florio was too unpopular and Eagleton was projecting too high a turnout of Democratic groups.[16]

By 1997, I was polling New Jersey again for the *New York Post* and, just as in the case of 1996, produced the only poll showing incumbent governor Whitman leading (and eventually beating) Democrat Jim McGreevey. Again, Eagleton did report that 11 percent of the voters were still undecided and that 16 percent said that they had in the past either made up their minds or changed their minds in the voting booth.[17]

Table 3.1.   NY Post/Fox 5 News/Zogby—New Jersey—November 2, 1997
N=619 MOE +/- 4.0 Percentage Points

	Total		North		Central		South	
	f	%	f	%	f	%	f	%
McGreevey	233	37.7	99	43.3	63	33.0	71	35.7
Whitman	244	39.4	89	39.0	78	40.9	77	38.5
Sabrin	24	3.9	4	1.6	9	4.8	12	5.8
NtSure	117	18.9	37	16.1	41	21.2	40	20.0
Total	619	100.0	228	100.0	191	100.0	199	100.0

	Democrat		Republican		Indep/Other	
	f	%	f	%	f	%
McGreevey	178	66.3	16	8.3	39	25.8
Whitman	36	13.5	149	74.8	59	38.9
Sabrin	3	1.0	7	3.7	14	9.4
NtSure	51	19.2	26	13.2	39	26.0
Total	268	100.0	199	100.0	152	100.0

(continued)

Table 3.1. NY Post/Fox 5 News/Zogby—New Jersey—November 2, 1997, Continued

	18–29		30–49		50–64		65+	
	f	%	f	%	f	%	f	%
McGreevey	32	33.5	86	36.1	65	44.6	49	37.5
Whitman	39	41.4	106	44.7	50	34.1	46	34.7
Sabrin	3	3.0	10	4.2	7	4.9	3	2.6
NtSure	21	22.1	36	15.0	24	16.4	33	25.3
Total	95	100.0	237	100.0	146	100.0	132	100.0

	Race									
	Total		Wh, non-Hisp		Hispanic		Afr American		Other/ Mixed	
	f	%	f	%	f	%	f	%	f	%
McGreevey	225	37.9	157	34.1	15	44.5	43	59.5	10	36.6
Whitman	238	40.0	193	41.9	17	50.4	15	21.4	12	45.1
Sabrin	23	3.9	23	5.1						
NtSure	108	18.2	88	19.0	2	5.1	14	19.1	5	18.4
Total	595	100.0	461	100.0	34	100.0	72	100.0	27	100.0

	Education							
	<HighSch		High Sch Grad		Some Coll		Coll Grad+	
	f	%	f	%	f	%	f	%
McGreevey	6	27.7	67	49.6	51	33.6	104	35.7
Whitman	7	31.9	36	27.1	64	41.8	133	45.6
Sabrin			6	4.4	9	5.8	10	3.3
NtSure	9	40.4	25	18.9	29	18.9	45	15.4
Total	23	100.0	135	100.0	152	100.0	291	100.0

	Race									
	Total		Wh, non-Hisp		Hispanic		Afr American		Other/ Mixed	
	f	%	f	%	f	%	f	%	f	%
VeryFav	144	24.2	122	26.4	12	35.2	6	8.1	4	16.1
SmwtFav	225	37.9	168	36.4	9	25.9	36	50.6	12	45.0
SmwtUnfav	99	16.6	80	17.4	8	23.0	7	9.1	4	14.9
VeryUnfav	106	17.9	77	16.7	4	10.9	19	26.1	7	24.0
NtFamiliar	7	1.1	7	1.4						
NtSure	14	2.3	8	1.7	2	5.1	4	6.1		
Total	595	100.0	461	100.0	34	100.0	72	100.0	27	100.0

	Education							
	<High Sch		High Sch Grad		Some Coll		Coll Grad+	
	f	%	f	%	f	%	f	%
VeryFav	6	26.5	21	15.6	32	21.1	87	29.8
SmwtFav	6	25.4	58	42.7	65	42.6	97	33.4
SmwtUnfav			16	11.6	25	16.6	59	20.1
VeryUnfav	4	18.6	36	27.0	28	18.5	40	13.6
NtFamiliar	2	10.2	2	1.3			3	.9
NtSure	4	19.3	3	1.9	2	1.1	6	2.2
Total	23	100.0	135	100.0	152	100.0	291	100.0
	Religion							
	Catholic		Protestant		Jewish		Other/ No Aff	
	f	%	f	%	f	%	f	%
VeryFav	66	25.3	48	26.9	5	12.9	21	18.2
SmwtFav	94	36.0	66	37.2	16	41.7	48	42.1
SmwtUnfav	42	16.1	28	15.8	11	26.6	17	14.7
VeryUnfav	45	17.3	29	16.1	6	14.6	29	25.0
NtFamiliar	5	2.0	2	1.3				
NtSure	8	3.2	5	2.8	2	4.2		
Total	260	100.0	178	100.0	40	100.0	114	100.0

One in five voters were still undecided on November 2 in our poll. One clue was that in that same poll, 22 percent of Black voters were undecided. Again, as noted above, that meant late in the game that many probably would not even bother to show up at the polls. Further disturbing evidence that McGreevey might lose was that 19 percent of Democrats were still not sure of their choice, compared with only 13 percent of Republicans. Women are normally critical to a Democrat's chances of winning, and our poll found 22 percent of women still unsure.

What was so wrong with the other New Jersey polls? First, it appears that their polling ended too early. With so many (and even growing numbers of) undecided voters, the races became more volatile. But no one dared to probe why these voters were undecided. Nor did it appear that pollsters would stay in the field trying to capture the last-minute break toward one candidate or the other. On the surface, that is okay. Extra polling means extra costs, and perhaps there wasn't sufficient money in the budget. Nor can polls be correct with pinpoint accuracy every time. There are late-deciding voters.[18] The problem is that the media reports which candidate is leading and runs with it as gospel, labeling the polling leader as such and reducing coverage of the struggling candidate who is behind. Eagleton, again to its credit, did report changes and possible red flags in these races, but voters shifted late and their poll simply did not catch the final break. So, there were really no Whitman or Torricelli surprises. Nor would there have been any last-minute GOP shock in 2021's gubernatorial race in New Jersey, which I will describe later.

Exhibit E: Howard Dean and the Myth of the Scream

In early December 2003, the Reuters/Zogby poll showed Howard Dean, governor of Vermont, with mammoth leads over Senators John Kerry and John Edwards, congressman Dick Gephardt, and others for the Democratic presidential nomination. We were polling likely Democratic caucus/primary voters nationwide as well as in Iowa, New Hampshire, and South Carolina. At that point, his lead in New Hampshire alone was thirty-five points! My previously noted colleague John Kenneth White discussed coauthoring a piece with me on why the Dean juggernaut could not be stopped. But we decided to hold off. Good judgment. What followed was nothing short of amazing.[19] Dean was pretty much running as a one-issue candidate: ending the growing war in Iraq, which was unpopular among Democrats.[20] We asked in our polling throughout 2003 who likely Democratic primary/caucus voters preferred: a nominee who stood on principle, or one who could defeat President George W. Bush. All year the principled nominee was preferred by a factor of two to one. And Dean was seen as that candidate.

On December 15, 2003, the world learned that the deposed leader of Iraq, Saddam Hussein, was captured. Our polling—and frankly everybody else's—had shut down for the holidays. We did not resume until January 3, 2004, and then continued with daily tracking of three-day rolling averages until the (very early) January 19 Iowa caucuses. Our first published results in the new year showed Dean's lead in the Hawkeye State leveling off and then declining by a point or two each day. He and Gephardt (from neighboring Missouri) were running negative ads against each other, and the latter's numbers were going down as well—as Kerry and Edwards each gained a small percentage with each passing day. By halfway through the tracking, Kerry pulled into the lead, with Edwards in second place, while Dean and Gephardt fell into third and fourth place, respectively.[21]

From the polling, we gleaned that there was now a complete reversal in voter sentiments among Iowa voters: they now, closer to caucus day, wanted someone who could defeat President Bush by a factor of two to one over the principled guy. Kerry and, to a slightly lesser degree, Edwards were the beneficiaries. Kerry, of course, won the caucuses and immediately won the "three *m*'s" reward of the Iowa caucuses: media, money, and momentum.[22] Kerry, who like Dean was a neighbor of New Hampshire, then won a big victory in that state's primary.

One of the myths that needs to be dispelled is that of Dean's "I Have a Scream" speech, which addressed his supporters on the night of the Iowa caucuses.[23] He was hyped up, almost manic, speaking to a large group, while the live microphones broadcast him yelling and hooting. Television commentators wrongly concluded that Dean's heat turned off potential supporters and killed his chances. Our polling was clear: all was already lost for him when Democratic supporters decided that he could not defeat the unpopular and failed incumbent president. As his numbers dropped in the Reuters/Zogby tracking in Iowa, our interviewers and Reuters journalists were reporting from follow-up calls to our respondents that Dean simply had too many volunteers going door-to-door encouraging people to vote in the caucuses, and the message was getting tiresome. We were hearing things like "We get it about the war, but what else does Dean believe in?" The polling captured this information all in real time, and Dean's candidacy was doomed long before he screamed into an open microphone.

Exhibit F: How Obama Won Reelection

Most observers have forgotten that the 2012 general election between President Barack Obama and Republican challenger Mitt Romney was a hotly contested horse race until the weekend before Election Day.[24] This time I was conducting daily tracking polls for the *Washington Times*. (I used to tell my liberal friends in New York that I had the "backward" *Times* and *Post* as clients, because they are the political opposites of their counterparts in New York and Washington.) The conservative newspaper in Washington, DC, had always believed in me and had featured my 1996 daily presidential polling on its front page when other media were still reticent about sharing the spotlight with their own internal numbers.

The 2012 election was not promising to be a runaway election for President Obama. My daily tracking showed the lead changing between Obama and former governor Mitt Romney several times as the candidates took turns opening up substantial leads. This same fluctuation was similar to what we had found in hard-fought battles like Gore versus Bush in 2000 and Kerry versus Bush in 2004, as well as even for a time in Obama versus McCain in 2008. What was going on this time was that President Obama had a rough first term. While he used his early congressional majority to push through a recovery bill that saved the United States from a depression and steered his own party to pass the historic

Affordable Care Act, his party was split in Congress between progressives and moderates (the latter called Blue Dog Democrats), and there was a growing sense of disappointment from his own base that he had come to office with so much promise (and so many promises) but could not deliver. Obama the incumbent was going to face a challenge from the last of the breed of moderate Republicans.

It did not help matters that Obama showed up ill prepared for his first debate with Romney, uncharacteristically tongue-tied, fatigued, and simply out of it. His performance was terrible, and Romney was, as always, sharp, prepared, and handsome as all hell. Obama's polling numbers dropped like an anvil from the sky.[25] Romney led by as much as seven points at one time in our tracking. What was happening with Obama and his formerly adoring public can be summed up in just one word: disappointment. We could add an adjective to "disappointment" as well: profound. The man who saved the nation from a depression and finally delivered on a law that every Democratic president had promised since Harry Truman—universal health insurance—was seen as ineffectual, someone who had falsely raised expectations that were impossible to deliver on and who was about to enter the lexicon of mediocre presidential leaders. The numbers were clear, especially among eighteen-to-twenty-nine-year-old voters, who had passionately believed in him and had given him 67 percent of their vote, not to mention a near-record turnout on top of that in 2008.[26]

Remember also that about 40 percent of this age cohort was nonwhite.[27] What was clear in our tracking was that while Obama was indeed winning among young voters, he was polling around only 55–56 percent of their support. Plus, there were substantial numbers who were still undecided. Once again, as noted before, they were not going to vote for a GOP candidate. That party had burned itself out for younger folks on social issues like abortion, gay rights, and marriage, to name a few. My October 19–20 *Washington Times*/Zogby poll showed Obama leading, as I wrote in *Forbes* on October 22, 2012:

> A new *Washington Times*/Zogby Poll of likely voters nationwide conducted this past weekend shows President Barack Obama now leading his GOP challenger Mitt Romney 50 percent to 47 percent.
>
> Mr. Romney now hits 58 percent among white voters, his best performance yet, but Mr. Obama is outperforming his 2008 showing by polling 40 percent. As I have written before, the former Massachusetts Governor must get an even larger share of whites to offset what will be a declining share of the total vote in 2012. Mr. Obama continues to consolidate his leads among Hispanics (74 percent–26 percent, larger than his 67 percent–31 percent victory in 2008) and African Americans (89 percent–6 percent, compared with 95 percent–5 percent in 2008).

But the next two weeks will all be about young voters and the President's anemic 11 point lead (54 percent–43 percent) is perhaps most of all for him. With two weeks to go, the only thing we know for sure is that we don't know for sure.[28]

By Friday before the election, I started to see Obama's overall support, especially among eighteen-to-twenty-nine-year-olds, move up as undecided voters started to make their decision. Here is what I wrote in a press release on October 2 (four days before the election):

> The governor (Romney) leads by only three points among independents and it's trending Obama. I wouldn't call this big momentum but . . . he was down three points three days ago and now he's up two. That is a five-point swing. At the same time, we do see him improving his numbers with young voters and hitting the 60 percent mark. And, of course, that's very significant. It doesn't match what he did last time (2008) but it's enough to put him in contention. And right now I wouldn't tell you to see your bookie with a thousand-dollar bet on Obama winning but it's certainly looking better, obviously, more competitive.

By Saturday, 60 percent of young voters were planning to vote for President Obama. What was especially striking was the trajectory of support among young women, who were by the weekend reaching the high sixties level. I wrote a piece for *Forbes* on Saturday titled "What If It Isn't So Close After All?"[29] Meaning that younger voters were deciding late in several key battleground states and tipping toward Obama. If this momentum continued, the popular vote would be a majority for Obama, and the electoral college would be a landslide.

Obama won reelection with 51.1 percent of the popular vote to Romney's 47.2 percent, 332 electoral votes to Romney's 206.[30] But amazingly, and clearly, from our tracking polls, Obama won with 73 percent of the vote among eighteen-to-twenty-nine-year-old women—a remarkable achievement. They also turned out in huge numbers.[31]

CHAPTER 4

Misreading What the Polls Are Really Saying

Why did Hillary Clinton really lose in 2016? Were there no clues along the way? Had she been stabbed in the back by FBI director James Comey, who released a memo about her violating the law in using her private email server to illegally possess classified documents at home? Was there a Russian conspiracy to elect a Russophile (or at least a Putin-phile) as president?[1] Once again, real answers come from scrutinizing the polling in the closing days of that race.

Too often, conventional wisdom on political winners and losers is formed among commentators and reporters who mainly talk to each other, form their own conclusions, and are too insular to be able to accept numbers and other facts that run contrary to their views. This is what I believe happened in 2016 regarding the Trump victory, as well as in the projection of a huge "red wave" in 2022. Polls suggested otherwise, but opinion leaders trusted themselves too much. We call it "confirmation bias," and if you are a Roman Catholic, this would be the eighth of what we could relabel as the "eight cardinal sins"—a close neighbor to sloth.

An honest reading of a poll should be independent and uncluttered by outside demands or mandates. As we look closely at the 2016 presidential table, there was plenty in the polls to suggest that Trump could win. It was not certain by any means, but neither was a Clinton victory in the bag. The press and punditry abrogated their duty to be honest brokers. It was then easy for them to spin the blame on the "polls" as the chief culprit. But the polls caught the more important message: follow the trend line. The polls did. The commentators did not.

Exhibit G: The Polls Were Actually Pretty Good in 2016

In the race between former Secretary of State Hillary Clinton and former billionaire Donald Trump, the polls were right and the pundits were dead wrong. Consider the data, please, and do note that I stayed out of this race, so I am reviewing the work of my colleagues in a favorable light. The leading association of US pollsters actually formed a committee to study why the polling failed.[2] As you'll see below, I don't think it did, and I was stunned that professional pollsters wasted time on something that didn't happen. It revealed to me that we pollsters had even set up impossible expectations for ourselves and missed the point that the polls had truly captured a very reasonable trend line. The conclusion of the AAPOR was that they really just didn't know what happened. In the public conversation it was a foregone conclusion that Clinton would win. Trump had surprised everyone by staying in the race so long, winning the primaries, defeating any challengers at the GOP convention, and uniting his party so solidly behind his candidacy. Nonetheless, polls showed throughout that only 36 percent of voters believed he told the truth in most instances.

Clinton struggled a bit more to rein in the progressive left, led by Senator Bernie Sanders, who had won a substantial number of primaries, caucuses, and delegates. In the end, the Democrats did get behind their standard-bearer, although enthusiasm levels were pretty low among some key groups. The chief problem she faced was that she never really bolstered her positive numbers and could not rally enough voters around her central theme: that it was her turn to be president. Trump's campaign was roiled right before the election by his own words on a 2007 videotape, bragging to a reporter for *Access Hollywood* (and a Bush family member no less) about his exploits and vulgar treatment of women, including physical assault.[3] At the same time, Clinton was stopped in her tracks by a letter from the FBI director saying that he would reopen his bureau's investigation of government emails that she sent from her home.[4] Frankly, neither candidate was truly beloved among a majority of voters.[5]

A look at the published polls from approximately ten days before Election Day tells a clear and obvious story of what happened to Clinton's campaign and how Trump won in the battleground states. First and foremost, let's dismiss any notion that the polls got the nationwide popular vote wrong. As you can see below, the final RealClearPolitics average had Clinton in the lead by 3.2 percentage points, whereas her actual victory margin was 2.1 percentage points. C'mon, give us all a break! That was pretty damned good.

Table 4.1. 2016 Presidential Polling—Clinton vs. Trump, RealClearPolitics Final Averages vs. Actual Results

Nationwide/ State	RCP Final Average	RCP Spread	Actual Result	Actual Spread	Polling Average by Date
Nationwide	Clinton 46.8– Trump 43.6	Clinton +3.2	Clinton 48.2– Trump 46.1	Clinton +2.1	10/21–10/31 (Clinton +2 to 10 points)
Arizona	Trump 45.8– Clinton 45.0	Trump +0.8	Trump 48.1– Clinton 44.6	Trump +3.4	10/20–10/28 (Trump +1 to 5 points)
Colorado	Clinton 43.3– Trump 40.4	Clinton +2.9	Clinton 48.2– Trump 43.3	Clinton +4.9	10/26–10/31 (Race tied to Clinton +3 points)
Georgia	Trump 49.2– Clinton 44.4	Trump +4.8	Trump 50.5– Clinton 45.4	Trump +5.1	10/20–10/30 (Trump +1 to 9 points)
Michigan	Clinton 45.4– Trump 42.0	Clinton +3.4	Trump 47.3– Clinton 47.0	Trump +0.3	10/23–10/30 (Clinton +6 to 8 points)
Nevada	Trump 45.8– Clinton 45.0	Trump +0.8	Clinton 47.9– Trump 45.5	Clinton +2.4	10/20–10/30 (Clinton -3 to +7 points)
New Hampshire	Clinton 43.3– Trump 42.7	Clinton +0.6	Clinton 46.8– Trump 46.5	Clinton +0.3	10/20–10/23 (Clinton +3 to 9 points)
North Carolina	Trump 46.5– Clinton 45.5	Trump +1.0	Trump 49.9– Clinton 46.2	Trump +3.7	10/20–10/26 (Clinton +1 to 7 points)
Pennsylvania	Clinton 46.2– Trump 44.3	Clinton +1.9	Trump 48.2– Clinton 47.5	Trump +0.7	10/23–10/25 (Clinton +7 to 11 points)
Virginia	Clinton 47.3– Trump 42.3	Clinton +5.0	Clinton 49.8– Trump 44.4	Clinton +5.4	10/20–10/30 (Clinton +4 to 12 points)
Wisconsin	Clinton 46.8– Trump 40.3	Clinton +6.5	Clinton 46.5– Trump 47.2	Trump +0.7	10/26–10/31 (Clinton +4 to 6 points)

As for the states, around ten days before the election, Clinton was up by as many as nine points in New Hampshire, eleven in Pennsylvania, eight and six each in Michigan and Wisconsin respectively, seven in North Carolina, and so on. While Comey's letter broke at that point, announcing that he would continue the investigation into her storing and communicating classified government information in her home, the earlier release of Trump's famous *Access Hollywood* tape in which he told reporter Billy Bush about his abuse of women may have already burned itself out. Trump did not move in the polls. His base remained solidly behind him. But Clinton really suffered, and this effect could be seen in the tracking polls in each of the battleground states. Slowly sliding a point or two each day from her leads, her numbers deteriorated to the point that the day before the election, she was tied in New Hampshire, leading by only three in Pennsylvania, up by only one in Michigan and Wisconsin, and down by three in North Carolina.[6] Again, Trump's base remained solid, although he did not look like he could win the national popular vote. But something was clearly going on in those battleground states. First, we saw young women—so vital to President Obama's reelection four years earlier—start to abandon Clinton and move into the undecided column in the final phase of the election.[7] Second was the bleeding of Black voters. The Sunday before the election, CBS News released its daily tracking poll in conjunction with YouGov. The headline they chose to feature was Clinton's insurmountable lead among Blacks—81 percent to 8 percent, with 11 percent undecided. This was seen only as it was on the surface, as a blowout for Clinton. Indeed, it was a big lead among a group vital to any Democratic victory. But it was woefully inadequate for a win. Barack Obama won 95 percent of the Black vote in his 2008 victory, and 93 percent in 2012.[8] [9] Besides, in 2008, the Black percentage of the total votes cast was 12.9 percent—2.9 percentage points higher than the 10 percent of the total they represented four years earlier. And in 2012, Black voters would represent 13.1 percent of the total votes cast.[10] With Obama winning more than nine in ten of those voters, that provided him with a huge advantage.

In 2016, the real question for me was why—according to CBS/YouGov—11 percent of Black voters were still undecided two days before the election. My experience on the ground and in polling suggested an answer: they were simply not going to vote. That is precisely what happened. While on Election Day, Clinton did in fact win 87 percent of the Black vote to Trump's 8 percent, Black voters represented only 12 percent of the total votes cast, compared with 13.1 percent of the total in 2012, the first time the percentage of Black voters had dropped in twenty years.[11] These missing Black votes also help explain what happened in battleground states with large numbers of Black registered voters like Pennsylvania, Michigan, Wisconsin, and North Carolina—all of which Clinton lost.

The polls were pretty good, for the most part. The aggregated average of nationwide polls gave Clinton the lead, with two pollsters—TIPP (TechnoMetrica Institute of Policy and Politics) on behalf of *Investors Business Daily* and ABC News—nailing the correct margin.[12] And the statewide battleground polls captured the accurate trend lines. A final poll result not getting the result to the exact percent is immaterial. What matters is whether it captures the vectors and the direction of where things are heading. That is why I felt comfortable writing in *Forbes* at noon on Election Day, "Be very careful of anyone who says he or she has it all figured out."[13]

Pollsters compile and comb through numbers. But we also talk to more people than anyone else. Our job is to be good with the numbers but also to have enough experience with individuals that we use their stories to complement those that emerge from the numbers. In October 2016, I spoke to a local mentoring class of "young scholars" at Utica College, now Utica University. These were middle-school and high-school teens from lower-income families in a college prep program. In my very diverse city of Utica, this group included children of Burmese, Bosnian, Sudanese, Ukrainian, and Syrian refugees. They wanted to discuss the election. A thirteen-year-old girl—a very talented artist, I should add—said, "I have only one thing to say. The US should have a woman President and it will. But just not this woman and not this time." There was my story that rounded out the data. In fact, her comment inspired an analytical piece I wrote for *Forbes* just after the 2016 election: "The Wrong Woman at the Wrong Time." As I wrote on November 9, the day after the election:

> This election was not a repudiation of the status quo or a rejection of "Barack Obama's third term." On the contrary, of those 140 million voters yesterday, 54 percent gave President Obama a positive job approval rating and more (31 percent) said they were doing better financially than said they were doing worse (25 percent). Indeed, my colleagues at PPP (a Democratic robo-polling firm) showed a little over two weeks ago that when Hillary Clinton was leading Donald Trump by just 2 points, Mr. Obama was leading 54 percent to 41 percent in a hypothetical matchup with Mr. Trump.
>
> Let's face it, this election was not supposed to be close. Democrats went into it with clear advantages: a popular President, an economy that was turning around, a recent Electoral College history that was frontloaded for Democrats, and an opposition in complete disarray. And she blew it. She did so by underperforming Mr. Obama. She only received 54 percent of 18–29-year-olds and 87 percent of a lower turnout of African Americans. In slam dunk Wisconsin, she only defeated Mr. Trump among 18–29-year-olds 46 percent–39 percent (Obama had received 60 percent four years ago).[14]

Following an Election Day evening of television appearances, I went back to my hotel room in DC around 11:30 and watched the analysts and anchors on both CBS and CNN looking flummoxed and pained that Donald Trump had actually been elected president. How could this outcome possibly have happened? Another lesson: When reading the polls, be sure to look for more than bytes of information that bolster your preconceived biases and assumptions. Again, I did not poll the 2016 cycle, but I have always been pained by the automatic, knee-jerk conclusion that the polls were wrong. They were good and plain as day in 2016.

Exhibit H: The Revolt of the Suburban Moms

The 2021 gubernatorial elections in Virginia and New Jersey seemed to also trip up both the pollsters and the media watchers. Public education has never been the top national issue since I started polling in 1984. In fact, it had really never been in even the top five issues in any election year, until 2021. The issue was thrust into the national limelight with the battle over racial justice following several high-profile police killings of unarmed Black suspects, notably the horrific videorecorded strangling of George Floyd in Minneapolis. Riots, aggressive demonstrations by Black Lives Matter, the shooting of demonstrators by a seventeen-year-old white man from out of state—all these hot actions led to a powerful countermovement by whites in cities and states across the country.[15] Whereas Democrats won back control in both chambers of Congress as a rejection of President Donald Trump's policies and rhetoric, and former Vice President Joe Biden won a decisive victory over Trump for the White House in 2020, public education became a dominant wedge issue in the important bellwether states of Virginia and New Jersey, where high-profile gubernatorial elections were held the first year after a presidential election.

In Virginia, former Governor Terry McAuliffe, a chief Democratic fundraiser for President Clinton and Democrats across the country, was challenged by wealthy and ultraconservative private-equity investor Glenn Youngkin. Virginia had been voting reliably Democrat in the past elections—Hillary Clinton defeated Trump 50 percent to 45 percent in 2016, while Joe Biden defeated him 54 percent to 44 percent in 2020. A new issue rose to the forefront: public schools and who gets to decide what children are taught. The issue began as part of the MAGA revolt against elites, with a large dose of racism. Parents were rebelling against critical race theory, which they claimed purports that the United States, both past and present, must in all things be viewed through a prism of racism. In fact, this theory is not taught anywhere in the United States, contrary to the alarmed assertions. The definition of critical race theory is, of course, more complex than what its detractors claimed, but that was their perspective.[16] Fueled by the 1619 Project led by the *New York Times* and several historians, the idea was to teach a more multicultural version of American history, one less white-centric and more critical of the role whites played in slavery, colonialism, and genocide of peoples of color.[17] Even though the 1619 Project has not really caught on, the opposition to liberal elites trying to thrust dogma on young people was just too much for suburban women and conservative activists. This was, to them, another example of remote elite educators teaching values inimical to traditional conservative values.[18]

Republican Glenn Youngkin rode this issue to victory over Terry McAuliffe. Youngkin was able to take votes from suburban moms, who had been giving Democrats their margin of victory in the previous decade and a half, and place them solidly in the GOP camp.

New Jersey's gubernatorial election turned out to be a shocker. There had never been any doubt that incumbent Phil Murphy would solidly defeat GOP challenger Jack Ciatterelli. All polls had Murphy with substantial leads of 6 to 9 percentage points heading into the election. Trafalgar Polling had it down to a four-point lead, but their results have generally been the most GOP-friendly and were thus considered an outlier. Murphy won by just three points, 51 percent to 48 percent. This low gap caught everyone by surprise, including Murphy's own pollster, Danny Franklin:

> There were historic surges in turnout in Republican counties. And not in Democratic counties. . . . This might sound kind of defensive, but the reason the polls showed majority support for Phil Murphy, and general agreement with his policies, and his approach to *COVID*, is because a majority of New Jerseyans do believe that. That's where the million-Democrat advantage shows up. It shows up in polls that are representative of New Jersey. But the actual turnout—and we'll know more about this as we learn more about who came out to vote and where—the actual turnout wasn't necessarily representative of that. That doesn't mean it was unrepresentative of what's going on. In every election, passion has a vote, and passion votes, and that's reflective of something real.[19]

Franklin went on to say that there was a late-breaking wave that caused higher Republican voter turnout. But then he threw his arms in the air, saying that polling can never catch or even assess what causes a late-breaking wave. Meanwhile, in a postelection op-ed, Patrick Murray, director of the Monmouth University Polling Institute, simply threw in the towel, saying that perhaps pre-election public polling should end because journalists want certainty and report polls as such. But they cannot always offer that kind of precision.[20]

It appears to me that both mea culpas are somewhat true, though they still missed the boat. We pollsters cannot promise exactitude in predicting the future.

And journalists and commentators should be smarter than that. But what we can do is offer the snapshot of the moment, the trend line of where things could be headed, a look at which voters may be turning or are losing interest and what is driving them. But even when we "leave the lights on" long enough, we may miss the unique phenomenon of the last-minute break.

Every one of the prominent polls in New Jersey once again stopped polling at least one week before the election. We have already seen the importance of last-minute decision-makers, especially in New Jersey. If polls are going to be used as predictive—and I do not believe they should!—then we must be fair to both the voting public and the pollsters and allow them the time and budget to continue the polls as long as they can. A pollster's accuracy is now being graded on any number of factors, including history and the results of his/her final poll. I was once given a grade based on online polling I conducted in the first week of October, a full month before the election in 2008. If we are going to continue to go that way (that is, grade pollsters on accuracy, but then blame polls for their inaccuracy), then we had better let pollsters go into the last minute. If not, then reporting should be filled with an analysis of potential surprises and the turnout models used.

After polling quite a few statewide elections in New Jersey and helping for nearly a decade to launch polling at Richard Stockton University in Atlantic City, another valuable lesson I learned is to not trust anyone's polling in that state but mine.

So what do I think really happened with suburban moms in 2021?[21]

The vote of suburban women has always been critical, especially for Democrats. When they share Democrats' priorities and turn out to vote, it's the difference between a margin of victory and losing seats. This is a swing vote, both suburban women in general and younger moms in particular. For suburban moms, the top concern is always safety and security for their children, and in campaigns this issue has been expressed in different ways. I think what happened in 2021 is their world turned upside down. There was great concern about equal justice, especially in the wake of the George Floyd murder with all of the surrounding debate and events. By 2021, suburban moms became overwhelmed by the coverage of violence in the streets. There was also a perception that state and school board officials were teaching programs like critical race theory, ones into which suburban moms felt they didn't have any input. In some cases, they became downright hostile. Much of this sense of powerlessness and alienation was also no doubt a result of massive school closings, mandates to wear masks in public, and the reality of both losing income because of layoffs and their children falling behind in learning—all as a result of the government response to the COVID-19 epidemic. Republicans were making some headway with the argument that as crime and heavy demonstrations were occurring, at the same time that moms felt insecure, the problem could be blamed on Democratically controlled city governments and school districts.

Clearly they were among the leading supporters of right-wing politicians and of school board officials. Others, by contrast, were just kind of caught up in the flow and the sense that the world was becoming less familiar to them. What was being taught in schools was not benefiting from their input in any way, and I think it was a revolt against elites. It was a political swing, and the timing was right in 2021. But as we'll see next in 2022, there is evidence that the pendulum did swing back.

The Potency of the Abortion and Election Denial Issues, 2022

The 2022 congressional elections defied history. Generally speaking, we know that there have been only three times since the Civil War when the party in the White House has actually gained seats in the first off-year election of a first-term president.[22] The most recent case had been George W. Bush and the run-up to the war in Iraq in 2002. Coming back to the 2022 congressional election, reelection polls showed that President Biden's approval numbers were stuck in the low forties, Americans were dealing with double-digit inflation for the first time in forty years, the president had been stymied in his efforts to pass his domestic agenda, and, at least to Republican voters, there was a widespread fear that America's standing overseas appeared to be at a low, although in fact it had picked up since 2020. Voters were consistently asked the top four issues on their minds, and the results were clear: inflation, public safety, abortion rights, and fear over the condition of our democracy.[23] Republicans were confident about their chances to take over both chambers of Congress.

Republicans were certain that Americans cared most deeply about inflation. After all, polling clearly showed that it was the number-one issue and, of course, inflation has an impact on everyone. Voters also gave Republicans higher marks than Democrats on handling inflation—but the national margins were only five points. Besides, an issue like inflation has several causes, and there is little that a president or Congress can do. The GOP promised tax cuts—which, according to this humble noneconomist, would be inflationary—and fiscal cuts to domestic programs. Good luck there. So, in fact, many voters were not sure what Republicans in Congress could actually do.[24]

Public safety was a powerful issue, and the GOP could score significant points by linking increased crime with Democratic-run cities and connecting riots with groups like Black Lives Matter. It also raised the specter of the near-fictitious "antifa," allegedly a small group of anarchist rabble-rousers who got too much credit for causing turmoil in the streets.[25] But blaming antifa as a conspiratorial terrorist group was a way to rally the passions of conservative base voters and frighten suburban women voters. It had a strong tinge of racism and, since the days of President Richard Nixon's "law and order" slogan, it was a way to appeal to whites and even some Blacks who were exhausted by a lack of a sense of safety.[26] Polling seemed to indicate that it was working for the GOP.

Meanwhile, Republican candidates and consultants strongly felt that the abortion issue—brought to a boiling point by the June 2022 Supreme Court *Dobbs v. Jackson* case striking down abortion protections under 1973's *Roe v. Wade*—would dissipate, and suburban women would return to the 2021 support they gave to the GOP. They also felt that the MAGA-driven 2020 election denial rhetoric had quieted down, and even the candidates who rose to prominence on that issue were not talking about it very much. Wow, were they wrong.

External Cataclysmic Events as Drivers of the Abortion Debate

A brief history of the abortion issue as a hot potato is in order.[27] Overall, and the analysis here seems to be my own, the issue of legalization of abortion comes to the forefront whenever there is some form of cataclysmic event. In 1973, after many states had passed abortion protections following the sad thalidomide tragedies of the 1960s, *Roe v. Wade* passed in the Supreme Court. Thalidomide had been an over-the-counter drug that was commonly used in Europe and the United States for a few conditions associated with pregnancy. By the early 1960s, it was being prescribed to relieve the symptoms of morning sickness and insomnia, until it was discovered to cause severely malformed babies.[28] Women were seeking abortions, and legal options were not available to them. The reaction to *Roe v. Wade* empowered "pro-life" leaders like Phyllis Schlafly to launch a nationwide "right-to-life" and largely antifeminist movement among women.[29] It became the top rallying cry for the burgeoning conservative movement, a marriage of both traditional family values and anti–government intervention in one issue.[30] They formed powerful third political parties in states like New York and were a force that could make or break candidates or actually elect others. While President Gerald Ford gave lip service to the pro-life movement, First Lady Betty Ford was among the most prominent spokespeople for a woman's right to choose an abortion. The movement's power culminated in the ascendancy of Ronald Reagan to the White House.[31] Majorities might still support a woman's right to choose, but intensity on the issue was on the other side through much of the 1980s and 1990s.

In 1998, very close to the congressional elections, the pendulum swung toward pro-choice. A prominent obstetrician-gynecologist of Niagara Falls, New York, Dr. Barnett Slepian, was assassinated by a gunman who shot through the window while he was in his living room.[32] Public revulsion was so high that many progressive Democrats, who had not been very supportive of moderate Senate candidates like Chuck Schumer in New York or John Edwards in North Carolina, came out to vote and gave unexpected victories to the Democrats.[33]

Within a few years, with the advice of überpollster/communications guru Frank Luntz, the abortion issue that took center stage was legislation to allow for "late-term abortions"—that is, abortions when a mother's life is in danger in the third trimester.[34] Luntz himself told me that he coined the term "partial-birth abortion," which became institutionalized in GOP communications on the issue. That term, accompanied by horrific photos and actual jars of late-term fetuses, dominated the debate and hardened both sides.[35] Following a strategy modeled after the NAACP Legal Defense Fund's successful campaign to end segregation of schools, the right-to-life movement launched initiatives to end legal abortions on a state-by-state level, which culminated within two decades by limiting, if not almost completely ending, abortions in over twenty states. This situation led to one of these pro-life states being able to present a challenge to *Roe v. Wade* before a much more sympathetic, conservative Supreme Court by 2022.[36]

The June 2022 *Dobbs v. Jackson* decision was then the next game-changing event in abortion history. As it turned out, abortion would continue to be the rallying cry and driver for Democrats, liberals, and young women voters in 2022. First, according to exit polls, while abortion overall was the second top issue for all voters at 27 percent (coming after the top issue, inflation, at 32 percent), it was by far the main issue among Democrats at 46 percent, followed by inflation at 15 percent and guns pretty much tied at 14 percent.[37] My son and business partner Jeremy Zogby did a poll of 1,250 independent likely voters in September 2022 in five battleground states—Arizona, Georgia, Pennsylvania, Ohio, and Wisconsin. A series of questions stated, "If a candidate . . . promised to [support a list of issues], would that make you more likely or less likely to vote for them?" A majority (56 percent) said they would be more likely to vote for a candidate who promised to support reinstating *Roe v. Wade*. Repeated claims of voter fraud by a candidate in those states was the biggest turnoff for independents, with 59 percent saying they would be less likely to vote for said candidate and 49 percent selecting "much less likely" alone.[38]

In short, those issues did not go away for Democrats and helped to persuade independents to vote Democrat. Exit polls nationwide showed that this group tilted toward the Democrats. Of those who voted for candidates for the House of Representatives, 61 percent felt that abortion should be legal either in all cases or in most cases, while 37 percent said no. A deeper dive reveals the difference in intensity of the two sides, with 39 percent of the total voters (85 percent of Democrats!) describing themselves as "angry" about the *Dobbs v. Jackson* decision and only 16 percent of the turnout (95 percent of Republicans) saying they were "enthusiastic."[39]

Why did abortion have such staying power throughout the campaign? What Republicans miscalculated is that voters may be angry and demand change, but they eschew turbulence and instability. It is also very clear that once voters have something, it is very difficult to take it away. The reality of the Dobbs decision is that women were being denied a right that they had possessed for fifty years, a protection that came with the reduction of fear. Even for those who were moderate on the issue, the impact of the Supreme Court decision was fear, real pain, and uncertainty about the future. Some GOP pollsters suggested in the closing days of the campaign that rural voters could be less enthusiastic about voting than in previous years because they had "won" on the issue of abortion with the Supreme Court decision. Thus, the analysis went on, there was really no reason for them to come out and vote. But this suggestion did not pan out. Of the total turnout, 17 percent was from rural areas, the same as the 2018 election, when there was a Democratic landslide, and just one point higher than the 2014 election, when the Republicans picked up thirteen seats.[40] Of those who voted in 2022 for the House, 60 percent identified themselves as favoring legalized abortion, while 37 percent wanted it to be illegal, in contrast to 66 percent to 25 percent in 2018 and 52 percent to 43 percent in 2014. Stated simply, Democrats came out to vote.

As for election denial, independents joined with Democrats in the fear that the familiar and the sacred—elections that produce gracious winners and losers—would now be gone. Overall, of those who voted in 2022, 61 percent felt that Joe Biden was the legitimately elected president of the United States, and 79 percent believed that elections were conducted fairly in their states in 2020.[41] Those two issues, especially appealing to independents, allowed the Democrats and Biden to defy history.

Once again, as in 2016, the pundits were way off, while the polls actually served us well. The data reveals an overall good day for polling in the key US Senate races.

Unlike 2016, when Donald Trump's support was underestimated in final polling, in 2022 the underestimation was actually on the Democratic side.

Table 4.2. 2022 U.S. Senate Polls, RealClearPolitics Final Averages vs. Actual Results

State	Final RCP	RCP Spread	Actual Results	Spread
Arizona	GOP 48.3/Dem 48.0	GOP +4.3	GOP 46.5/Dem 51.4	Dem +4.9
Nevada	GOP 48.8/Dem 45.4	GOP +3.4	GOP 48.0/Dem 48.9	Dem +0.9
Pennsylvania	GOP 47.2/Dem 46.8	GOP +0.4	GOP 46.3/Dem 51.2	Dem +4.9
Georgia	GOP 47.2/Dem 46.8	GOP +0.4	GOP 48.5/Dem 49.4	Dem +0.9
New Hampshire	GOP 47.3/Dem 48.7	Dem +1.4	GOP 44.4/Dem 53.5	Dem +9.1
North Carolina	GOP 51/Dem 44.8	GOP +6.2	GOP 50.5/Dem 47.3	GOP +3.2
Wisconsin	GOP 50.2/Dem 46.6	GOP +3.6	GOP 50.4/Dem 49.4	GOP +1.0
Ohio	GOP 51.8/Dem 43.8	GOP +8.0	GOP 53.2/Dem 46.7	GOP +6.5
Colorado	GOP 44.3/Dem 50.0	Dem +5.6	GOP 41.3/Dem 55.9	Dem +14.6
Washington	GOP 46.3/Dem 49.3	Dem +3.0	GOP 42.6/Dem 57.1	Dem +14.5
Florida	GOP 52.4/Dem 43.6	GOP +8.8	GOP 57.7/Dem 41.3	GOP +16.4

Lessons from Chapter 4

Don't be a victim of myopia and insularity. Too often people involved in corporate and political campaigns spend their time talking to each other and to themselves. You, the pollster or the reader of the polls, are the one paid (hopefully, and also hopefully on time!) to speak to the public, hundreds and thousands of them. You carry a lot of power because of this arrangement, just like the talking heads on cable television and the networks did in 2016. They hated Donald Trump so much (a sentiment he was able to exploit to his own benefit) that they could not get their minds around a possible Trump victory. Don't fall victim to that shortcoming. Above all, do not get caught up in the spin of either side. If one side makes a statement—for example, in 2022 the shrinking rural voter or the missing continuing anger over the Dobbs abortion decision—check it out. Find the evidence for yourself.

If the overall numbers in a poll are ambiguous, is there any evidence among subgroups that suggests an undercurrent? Instead of looking only at the "agree/disagree" or "support/oppose" responses, do you see any clues in the more intense results—the "strongly agree/strongly disagree" answers—that can point to greater emotions driving a result? Jump around to other polls to see whether there are consistencies or inconsistencies on the issues that offer a clue to sentiments and drivers of decisions. If you are doing a poll, what are the other pollsters not asking? Even though a lot of my political polling over the years was for public use—media clients, lobbying groups, donors—I always tried to use the methods and questions of private pollsters and strategists to get deeper into the voters' minds. Good polling does not involve one-dimensional, totally neuter, ultimately meaningless questions and responses. It tries to attach each question to a real set of values to see what people cherish, detest, believe, or reject. Attitudes and opinions are legitimate, but they may be fleeting. Seeking to find core values tells us much more about the sample we are polling. It is very significant that only a little over a third trusted Hillary Clinton to tell the truth, just a day before the election. They didn't trust Donald Trump any more, but that was enough of a clue to cast doubt. Our polling in 2022 said that independents in battleground states were more turned off by election deniers than anything else. That, in itself, was plenty to cast doubt on Republican pollsters who were "predicting" a massive red wave.[42]

CHAPTER 5

Reading Polls from the Bottom Up

I have found it useful over the years to look at the internals of polls before I even consider the overall topline numbers. Translated, this means that we can glean a lot about what a poll is really telling us by looking at key subgroups. These can include the obvious demographics like men and women, age cohorts, racial identification, religious groups, and so on. At times I have found it extremely enlightening to create new groupings, like Weekly Walmart Shoppers, Investor Class, NASCAR Fans, and the Creative Class.[1] It is a very valuable tool to use if we let people identify themselves, because that tells us a lot about what is important to them and how they will decide and behave. I have written previously in my 2008 book, *The Way We'll Be: The Zogby Report on the Transformation of the American Dream,* that voters may be Catholic or older or female parents, but being a member of the National Rifle Association or a union member or living in a household in which there is a veteran could be a more accurate way of determining how they think and how they will vote.[2]

As for the types of groups I have created, the Weekly Walmart Shopper was reliably a conservative voter in the bag for President George W. Bush in 2000 and 2004 but shifted over to Barack Obama by 2008.[3] Why? Perhaps because Walmart made aggressive moves to locate in inner cities during that decade and thus picked up support among people of color. Probably also because younger voters, who had told us they would not be caught dead in a Walmart because it was so déclassé, found themselves increasingly relying on "Everyday Low Prices" once the Great Recession of 2008 and 2009 hit. The Investor Class is something I helped establish with the help of conservative antitax leader Grover Norquist in the late 1990s. Norquist is not someone with whom I agree on a lot of things; however, he is a very important figure in the conservative movement and has always been very respectful to me and my work. On a personal level, I believe he has been a courageous voice in the GOP by promoting more party outreach to

55

the growing US Muslim population. He has received a lot of flak from outright racists for this position.

My polling found that, as just one example, two men could have identical demographics, annual incomes, and similar portfolios, but the one who agreed that he was a "member of the Investor Class" was ten to twelve points more likely to vote for Republicans and identify as a conservative. That sentiment is the same today, except that the self-identified members of the Investor Class shrank dramatically during and after the Great Recession. NASCAR voters had heavily supported Bush and then Obama, the latter reflecting many things: that this group has a high percentage of women, that they were ready for change, and that there was a disproportionate loss of life and limb among their loved ones from the failed war in Iraq.

Table 5.1.   Reuters/C-SPAN/Zogby International Poll of Nationwide Likely Voters, October 31–November 3, 2008
MOE +/- 2.9 Percentage Points

	Region									
	Total		East		South		Central		West	
	f	%	f	%	f	%	f	%	f	%
Obama	663	54.1	185	66.2	161	50.4	203	53.5	114	46.3
McCain	523	42.7	93	33.4	149	46.7	164	43.2	116	47.3
Nader	10	.8	0	.1	1	.4	2	.5	7	2.8
Barr	13	1.0			5	1.4	7	1.9	1	.4
McKinney	6	.5			1	.4	1	.2	5	1.9
Other	10	.8	1	.3	2	.8	3	.8	4	1.4
Total	1225	100.0	279	100.0	319	100.0	380	100.0	247	100.0

	Party Recoded					
	Democratic		Republican		Independent	
	f	%	f	%	f	%
Obama	426	90.8	56	12.6	181	58.5
McCain	37	7.9	378	84.7	108	34.9
Nader	2	.4	6	1.4	2	.7
Barr	0	.1	4	.9	8	2.7
McKinney	1	.1			6	1.9
Other	3	.7	2	.5	4	1.4
Total	469	100.0	447	100.0	309	100.0

Table 5.2.   Reuters/C-SPAN/Zogby International Poll of Nationwide Likely Voters, October 31–November 3, 2008
MOE +/– 2.9 Percentage Points, Multi Candidate (set 1 of 3)

| | Likelihood | | | | | | Register to vote in last 6 mo? | | | |
| | Already Voted | | V Lkly | | Smw Lkly | | Yes | | No/NS | |
	f	%	f	%	f	%	f	%	f	%
Obama	193	55.9	455	53.2	15	59.7	115	64.0	548	52.4
McCain	147	42.5	370	43.3	6	23.5	62	34.4	461	44.1
Nader	2	.6	7	.9	1	3.5	2	1.4	8	.8
Barr			13	1.5					13	1.2
McKinney	1	.3	3	.4	2	7.5			6	.6
Other	2	.6	6	.7	1	5.8	1	.3	9	.9
Total	345	100.0	856	100.0	25	100.0	180	100.0	1046	100.0

| | Gender | | | | | |
| | Total | | Male | | Female | |
	f	%	f	%	f	%
Obama	663	54.1	303	49.8	361	58.4
McCain	523	42.7	285	46.8	238	38.6
Nader	10	.8	7	1.2	3	.5
Barr	13	1.0	8	1.4	4	.7
McKinney	6	.5	3	.4	4	.6
Other	10	.8	2	.4	7	1.2
Total	1226	100.0	608	100.0	617	100.0

| | AgeGroup-B | | | | | | | | | |
| | 18–24 | | 25–34 | | 35–54 | | 55–69 | | 70+ | |
	f	%	f	%	f	%	f	%	f	%
Obama	42	72.9	154	60.5	263	51.7	116	47.4	71	52.9
McCain	13	22.5	89	35.1	236	46.4	117	47.9	61	45.5
Nader			5	1.9	1	.1	3	1.2	1	.8
Barr			5	2.1	3	.5	3	1.4		
McKinney	3	4.7	1	.5	2	.4			1	.5
Other					4	.8	5	2.0	0	.3
Total	58	100.0	254	100.0	509	100.0	244	100.0	134	100.0

Table 5.2.   Reuters/C-SPAN/Zogby International Poll of Nationwide Likely Voters, October 31–November 3, 2008
MOE +/– 2.9 Percentage Points, Multi Candidate (set 2 of 3)

	Race									
	White		Hisp		Afr Amer		Asian		Other	
	f	%	f	%	f	%	f	%	f	%
Obama	409	44.9	76	64.2	134	98.5	18	73.6	20	82.5
McCain	473	52.0	35	29.3	1	.7	7	26.4	4	16.2
Nader	5	.5	5	4.3					0	1.4
Barr	10	1.1								
McKinney	4	.4	3	2.3						
Other	9	.9			1	.8				
Total	910	100.0	119	100.0	136	100.0	25	100.0	24	100.0

	AgeGroup									
	Total		18–29		30–49		50–64		65+	
	f	%	f	%	f	%	f	%	f	%
Obama	646	53.8	145	66.6	260	52.1	142	49.8	99	50.0
McCain	516	43.1	62	28.5	228	45.7	133	46.7	93	47.1
Nader	9	.8	5	2.2			3	1.1	2	.8
Barr	11	1.0	3	1.5	5	.9	2	.8	2	.8
McKinney	6	.5	3	1.2	3	.6			1	.4
Other	10	.8			3	.6	5	1.6	2	1.0
Total	1199	100.0	218	100.0	498	100.0	285	100.0	198	100.0

	Ideology						Union			
	Liberal		Moderate		Conservative		Yes		No/NS	
	f	%	f	%	f	%	f	%	f	%
Obama	266	91.9	225	64.9	117	22.8	198	66.6	465	50.1
McCain	15	5.2	115	33.2	375	73.0	94	31.5	429	46.3
Nader	1	.4	2	.4	8	1.5	0	.1	10	1.1
Barr			3	.9	9	1.8	0	.1	12	1.3
McKinney	6	2.0	1	.2			3	.9	4	.4
Other	2	.5	1	.3	5	.9	2	.8	7	.8
Total	289	100.0	346	100.0	514	100.0	298	100.0	928	100.0

Table 5.2.   Reuters/C-SPAN/Zogby International Poll of Nationwide Likely Voters, October 31–November 3, 2008
MOE +/– 2.9 Percentage Points, Multi Candidate (set 3 of 3)

	Religion											Born Again			
	Total		Catholic		Protestant		Jewish		Other/None			Yes		No/NS	
	f	%	f	%	f	%	f	%	f	%		f	%	f	%
Obama	658	54.1	183	55.9	274	45.1	23	64.5	178	72.6		92	33.3	181	54.8
McCain	520	42.8	131	40.1	322	53.0	12	33.0	55	22.3		178	64.5	144	43.6
Nader	10	.9	7	2.0	2	.3	1	2.4	1	.5		1	.5	0	.1
Barr	12	1.0	2	.7	5	.9			4	1.8		2	.8	3	.9
McKinney	6	.5	1	.2					6	2.3					
Other	10	.8	4	1.1	5	.8			1	.5		2	.9	2	.7
Total	1216	100.0	327	100.0	608	100.0	36	100.0	245	100.0		276	100.0	331	100.0

	Income											
	< $25K		$25–35K		$35–50K		$50–75K		$75–100K		$100K+	
	f	%	f	%	f	%	f	%	f	%	f	%
Obama	86	68.3	57	58.8	75	49.0	132	50.0	84	50.6	154	53.6
McCain	33	26.1	38	39.6	72	47.3	128	48.4	75	45.6	132	45.7
Nader	2	2.0			0	.2	1	.4			0	.1
Barr			1	1.0	3	2.1			4	2.3		
McKinney	3	2.0					3	1.0				
Other	2	1.6	1	.6	2	1.4	0	.2	2	1.5	2	.5
Total	125	100.0	96	100.0	153	100.0	265	100.0	165	100.0	288	100.0

Obama overperformed expectations for a Democrat with NASCAR fans, as he did among the mainly conservative group of self-described Investor Class voters. He also did very well with Catholics and moderates.

I had a section on "Retail Politics" in *The Way We'll Be* laying out the political spectrum of ideological/partisan identification among voters who preferred major big box stores.[4] All the way on the right, back then, were Walmart shoppers, followed in order by Sears and JC Penney folks toward the center-right. Progressive/very liberal shoppers preferred Neiman Marcus to Bloomingdale's, with Target occupying the center. But that was then. All these groups are up for grabs today. One of our future planned studies is a detailed look at online shopping outlets to see where at-home shoppers are today in their political preferences.

Below are two solid examples of taking data from a poll and finding an entirely new and different story that helped me explain what was likely to happen.

1999 New Hampshire and the Phenomenon of John McCain

A year before the New Hampshire primary, I again joined with Reuters to do a "campaign managers" poll—in other words, a public poll conducted the way private polls are normally done. So of course we tested in the GOP primary all of the stated candidates by name. Not surprisingly, the hottest name in the party those days was the new governor of Texas, George W. Bush. There were also some very big names like Secretary of Transportation Elizabeth Dole, former vice president Dan Quayle, former secretary of housing and urban development and football great Jack Kemp, and iconoclastic Arizona senator John McCain. There were a total of eleven. Naturally, Bush came in first, followed by Dole, McCain, Quayle, and Kemp. This result was due to two factors in particular. The first was that Bush had received pretty much all of the buzz following the 1996 election. He was the scion of the best-known Republican family, which led to the second reason—namely, there was still a considerable amount of confusion between his father (the former president) and himself. In this very same poll, we asked why voters made their choice, and 13 percent of *Governor* Bush's supporters told us, "He had been a good president and was robbed by Bill Clinton." The other top-tier candidates also benefited from name recognition.

Table 5.3.   Reuters/Zogby—New Hampshire Poll—April 19, 1999, Actual Candidate Names, Weighted Republicans N=309, MOE +/- 5.7 Percentage Points

Q: Republican presidential nomination: George W. Bush, Dan Quayle, Steve Forbes, Bob Smith, John Kasich, Lamar Alexander, Alan Keyes, John McCain, Gary Bauer, Pat Buchanan, and Elizabeth Dole—for whom would you vote?

		Frequency	*Valid Percent*
Valid	Bush	119	38.4
	Quayle	26	8.4
	Forbes	19	6.3
	Bob Smith	11	3.7
	Kasich	3	1.0
	Alexander	5	1.5
	Keyes	6	1.9
	McCain	28	8.9
	Bauer	2	.5

		Frequency	Valid Percent
	Buchanan	18	5.8
	Dole	46	14.9
	NS	26	8.6
	Total	308	100.0

But again, I was more interested with one year to go in which candidates had the strongest potential in New Hampshire. In other words, I wasn't thinking simply about what existed today but was looking to project what could happen in a year. The poll featured one of my favorite techniques, the "blind biography," allowing voters to choose the values and positions of the candidates without being biased by their names or parties. In the technique of "blind biographies," we offer a positive paragraph about each candidate, allowing for symmetry among candidates and not including their names. The data below shows how radically different the results came in.

I'm going to read you short biographies of the possible Republican candidates. Please tell me which one you would vote for if the primary were held today.

Candidate A is a former Reagan White House counsel and is founder of a conservative organization, the Family Research Council, which promotes family values, strongly opposes US policy with China, and has strong support from Christian conservatives.

Candidate B is a senator from a western state and, while conservative on most issues, is widely regarded as an independent within the Republican Party. He is a decorated Vietnam War hero and was a prisoner of war. He strongly believes in campaign finance reform and took on the big tobacco companies.

Candidate C is a former senator from the Midwest and a former vice president. He has strong support from Christian conservatives and is credited with first raising the issue of family values on the national stage. He has foreign policy experience.

Candidate D is governor of a large southern state, having been just reelected with nearly 70 percent of the vote. He has a strong record on taxes and education and calls himself a "compassionate conservative." He has strong appeal among Hispanics and women. He is pro-life but says that now is not the time to change the existing laws.

Candidate E is a congressman from the Midwest and chairs the House Budget Committee. While he backs tax cuts, he is especially concerned that the United States does not get back to large budget deficits. He is a strong defender of the recent budget deal that calls for large amounts of the surplus being used to shore up Social Security. He is youthful and projects an energetic image.

Candidate F is a former southern governor and Reagan administration secretary of education and college president. He is a moderate who favors abolishing teachers' unions and eliminating the capital gains tax. He is emphasizing his non-Washington administrative experience and personal character.

Candidate G is a former Reagan and Bush administration cabinet member and president of the Red Cross. She is pro-life, a born-again Christian, and a seasoned campaigner on the national level.

Candidate H is a wealthy publisher who is a strong critic of the IRS and proponent of the flat tax. He has recently moved beyond his economic proposals and emphasizes his strong position against abortion.

Candidate I is a former advisor to both Presidents Nixon and Reagan. He writes a newspaper column and is a television commentator. In addition to stressing his strong anti-abortion position, he is very opposed to free trade agreements and involvements in international situations in which US interests are not directly affected.

Candidate J is a former ambassador and has a national talk radio show. He is an ardent critic of abortion and perhaps the most dynamic speaker in the campaign.

Candidate K is a senator from New England. A former teacher, he stresses his conservative credentials and his experience as a strong critic of the Clinton administration in the Senate.

Table 5.4.   Reuters/Zogby—New Hampshire Poll—April 19, 1999
MOE +/- 5.7 Percentage Points, Weighted
Republicans N=309

		Frequency	Valid Percent
Valid	A	31	10.0
	B (McCain)	59	19.2
	C	32	10.3
	D (Bush)	75	21.1
	E	8	2.4
	F	5	1.6
	G	24	7.7
	H	13	4.3
	I	11	3.6
	J	5	1.8
	K	3	1.1
	None	73	13.9
	Total	309	100.0

Bush dropped fourteen points, to 24 percent, and McCain rose well above the second tier, up to nineteen points. McCain's biography was very compelling, and it was not a shock to me at all that within hours of the story hitting the Reuters wire I received a call from Rick Davis, McCain's longtime campaign strategist. It was also not so curious that about ten months later the McCain campaign ran ads showing the former POW on a gurney in Vietnam in black-and-white film saying, "They broke both my legs." Other ads declared him a maverick within the party, which was very reassuring to independent voters in this "live free or die" state. I note below that McCain won by eighteen points.

The McCain–Bradley Independent Primary in New Hampshire

Even though moderate conservative Republican senator John McCain and moderate liberal Democratic former senator Bill Bradley ran in their own party primaries in 2000, they were vying for the same voters in the New Hampshire primary. The two candidates had the broadest appeal to independent voters. We did a poll for Reuters right before the New Hampshire vote, and I published an op-ed for the *New York Times* on January 19, 2000.[5] Here are some examples from that poll.

Candidate A has a detailed health plan that includes spending billions from the projected budget surplus. Candidate B seems to avoid any detailed discussion of health reform.

Candidate A voted against the Persian Gulf War and recoils from unilateral intervention abroad. Candidate B supported the Gulf War and called for ground troops in Kosovo. Candidate A voted against welfare reform in 1996; Candidate B voted for it.

Candidate A is aloof, private, and intellectual in demeanor; he won't even answer innocuous questions, like what his favorite book is. Candidate B is an open book who is happy to dissect his personal flaws.

These statements briefly and adequately represented the views and personalities of the two men in New Hampshire. Bradley was "Candidate A" in the first and third sets; McCain was "Candidate A" in the middle set. We focused on independents because they can represent up to 40 percent of the total vote in both primaries.[6] Both men were running against the established candidates in their own parties—Bradley against Vice President Al Gore, while McCain was challenging Governor George W. Bush.

This poll—and others as we continued to track the results daily—revealed that these two men were fishing in the same pond. Each drew more support from independents than from his own party's voters. Among independents who said they would vote in the Democratic primary, 55 percent supported Bradley; 35 percent backed Al Gore. Among independents who said they would vote in the Republican primary, 48 percent backed McCain; only 31 percent favored Bush. Beyond the issues, what did New Hampshire independent voters really care about? They told us they just wanted a different kind of leader from President Clinton. Though generally happy after eight years of peace and prosperity, they preferred someone who "tells them the truth and who is willing to defy the establishment."[7] Hence the popularity of plainspoken mavericks like McCain and Bradley.

So, while they differentiated themselves from rivals in their own parties, McCain the conservative Republican and Bradley the liberal Democrat were competing against each other for the deep pool of independent voters. Indeed, the real wild card in that primary was the unofficial race between these two remarkably different candidates who needed to appeal to the same voters to win.

A few days before the primary, I saw Bradley move from within four points of Gore to a near collapse of support by primary day. Meanwhile, McCain was slowly pulling ahead of Bush. Bradley suffered a solid defeat, while McCain won by eighteen points. What happened? Independent voters must declare their intention to vote in a specific primary on the day itself. Much of Bradley's initial independent support went over to the maverick former prisoner of war. It was indeed an "off the radar" primary among independents. Our decision to focus on this pivotal group paid off for us.

Lessons from Chapter 5

The "Bradley–McCain primary" was unique enough to allow me to get an opinion piece published in the *New York Times*—always a good thing. But beyond that, it taught me to look past the obvious, to try to see things that others could be missing. A good pollster needs to be able to find the story behind the numbers, to look where no one else is going to look.

Several years later, when I contracted with Random House to do my first book on polling and what it says about the future, I was able to take a long view of my work over the years and identify trends and groups that I had not really had the time to see before. I found the Secular Spiritualists, who decided that they no longer wanted their lives consumed by owning the most things. There were the First Globals, the name I gave to Millennials who were transcending national boundaries in their friendships, travel, values, and entertainment. I discovered the Investor Class, whose self-identification set them apart from people who shared their demographic profile. Later, I would be able to use the process of self-identification to afford people the opportunity to define their own "neo-tribes."[8]

Numbers produce stories. Imagination and hard work help us to find the stories behind the numbers. My advice is to get inside the poll first. Go deep, well beyond the simple one-dimensional result covered on television. Whether crafting a poll or reading it, list upfront what you really need to get out of it. Don't rely only on the head-to-head result. Where can you find what is dear to people in the sample? Which issues are most important, but which are the sleepers among subgroups? In 2020, younger voters were least trustful of government, but they voted Democrat because racial justice and climate change were high on their list. So, too, was student loan forgiveness. This is not unlike older voters who tilt conservative and Republican but don't dare touch Social Security or Medicare.

Check to make sure the demographics look right. Do the party identification numbers seem accurate, especially considering recent exit polls? How do party identification and other demographics stack up with the numbers from other polls? Is there anything surprising or counterintuitive? Can these numbers be validated by other sources? Discuss the questionable results or demographics with colleagues before making any judgment.

What questions do any of the results raise for further pursuit? I have been doing polling professionally for a very long time, and yet each time I have examined my own results, there are at least a dozen (sometimes many more) questions I wish I had asked.

Don't treat any poll as a one-off. As in any research project, polls and individual questions are pathways for further inquiry. Just because the media or your own immediate needs may force emphasis on one or two findings, an end user should go beyond the simplistic conclusion, "What did this poll teach me?" Even better: "What didn't this poll answer?"

It also is not a bad thing if the response to a poll appears to make perfect sense. Try to leverage more from the data by asking why it makes sense.

And don't be afraid to be original, to take a different look than others do. Good data is vital; it is what solid researchers do and clients need. But it is not the end product. It is a means to an end, and, above all, it must be useful.

CHAPTER 6

The Aggregation-Industrial Complex

While I was working on this manuscript, someone misread this chapter's title as "The Aggravation-Industrial Complex," and it is. In the last decade or so, an entire new industry has been spawned by analysts who closely follow polls. Essentially, instead of relying on one, two, or five polls, websites like RealClearPolitics (RCP) and FiveThirtyEight (538) have brought the world of data analytics into the observation and projection side of polling. Beyond simply following and reporting new polls when these are available, these aggregators take the science side of data crunching, aggregate polls together, apply weighting mechanisms to certain pollsters according to their track records, and make daily projections on winners and losers in elections. Since there is much more public polling available than when I first started, there is of course a wide variety of polling methodologies and results. The theory behind aggregation is actually solid. Instead of relying on one poll or another, as in the old days, we place most of them in a cauldron, and in this era of big data we make some sense by averaging, applying weights for pollster track records, and creating unique formulas depending on the time of year, the quality of the sample, and so on.

I find this process fascinating for a few reasons. First, it is indeed a worthy effort to take lots of data from polls, make sense out of it, and then provide an easy-to-read capsule of where a political race or a job approval rating stands. The aggregators also have a good number of writers who provide historical context for both the numbers and their analysis to make things interesting. The practice carries polling to a whole new level, and I support innovation. Second, it produces a user-friendly model that is straightforward to read, follow, and discuss. The Jesuits say *utraque unum* ("out of many, one"), which works. I even used it for the title of my 2016 book, *We Are Many, We Are One: Neo-Tribes and*

Tribal Analytics in 21st-Century America. Overall, the aggregators have a decent track record, but there are truly problems with their output. In the name of full disclosure, I came out early in 2004 with online polls, and even though mine are still among the most accurate (see data below), we struggled out of the gate. Nate Silver of 538 and I also had conflicts when he ran some of my early polling in 2008 as final. In fact, I've had public battles with 538, and RCP still refuses to use my poll numbers.[1] CNN, NBC, and ABC and I have also had our disagreements, which is normal in the combative polling field generally, but if you consult the charts below, you will see how my numbers stack up.

Despite efforts by 538 to weight the value of polling companies based on their history of accuracy, RCP appears merely to apply a simple average of polls. The problem with both is that they tend to mix partisan pollsters—that is, those who work mainly with candidates and interest groups from one party or the other—together into one average batch with independent public pollsters like myself.[2] If we just compare RCP final averages in the 2022 cycle with the actual final election results in November 2022, we see a few problems right away. As we can observe below, RCP did pretty well in its averaging of the nationwide outcome in the 2020 presidential race, although several of its polls were way off. Most of the polls appear to have represented the final outcome within the margin of error. Also, please note that RCP did not include the John Zogby Strategies poll in its aggregation. For the record, when we initially began our online work in 2020, ours underrepresented the support for both Biden and Trump by two and three points. However, we were very close on the final spread between the candidates.

Table 6.1. Final Poll vs. Actual Results, 2020

Results	Date	Sample	MoE	Biden (D)	Trump (R)	Spread
Final Results	—	—	—	51.4	46.9	Biden +4.5
RCP Average	10/25–11/2	—	—	51.2	44.0	Biden +7.2
John Zogby Strategies	10/30–11/1	1000 LV	3.2	48.8	43.6	Biden +5.2
Economist/YouGov	10/31–11/2	1363 LV	3.3	53	43	Biden +10
IBD/TIPP	10/29–11/2	1212 LV	3.2	50	46	Biden +4

Results	Date	Sample	MoE	Biden (D)	Trump (R)	Spread
Reuters/IPSOS	10/29–11/2	914 LV	3.7	52	45	Biden +7
CNBC/Change Research (D)	10/29–11/1	1880 LV	2.3	52	42	Biden +10
Rasmussen Reports	10/28–11/1	1500 LV	2.5	48	47	Biden +1
Quinnipiac	10/28–11/1	1516 LV	2.5	50	39	Biden +11
JTN/RMG/Research	10/29–10/31	1200 LV	2.8	51	44	Biden +7
NBC News/Wall St. Journal	10/29–10/31	1000 RV	3.4	52	42	Biden +10
SurveyUSA	10/29–10/31	1265 LV	3.2	52	44	Biden +8
FOX News	10/27–10/29	1246 LV	2.5	52	44	Biden +8
Harvard-Harris	10/27–10/28	LV	—	54	46	Biden +8
The Hill/HarrisX	10/25–10/28	2359 LV	2.0	49	45	Biden +4
Emerson	10/25–10/26	1121 LV	2.8	50	45	Biden +5

By contrast, the RCP average—hence the individual polls included in the averaging—clearly underrepresented the Trump vote by almost three points.

The RCP averages in the battleground states tell a far different story from the national average. In eight of the nine states, Trump's count was understated—and in some instances, like Wisconsin (six points), Florida (four), Iowa (six), and Ohio (seven), greatly underrepresented. Some Republicans had suggested throughout the 2020 campaign that there was a hidden Trump vote among Republicans, Democrats, and independents who were possibly ashamed to admit to strangers on the phone that they were voting for him.[3] But I have always found Republicans less willing to talk to pollsters.

However, when we look closely at the battleground states in the 2022 United States Senate races, we find a different story, one in reverse. There is a tendency in the final RCP averages to underrepresent the support for the Democratic candidates.

Table 6.2. 2020 Presidential Polling—Biden vs. Trump, RealClearPolitics Final Averages vs. Actual Results; johnzogbystrategies.com

State	Final RCP	RCP Spread	Actual Results	Spread
Arizona	GOP 48.3/Dem 48.0	GOP +0.3	GOP 46.5/Dem 51.4	Dem +4.9
Nevada	GOP 48.8/Dem 45.4	GOP +3.4	GOP 48.0/Dem 48.9	Dem +0.9
Pennsylvania	GOP 47.2/Dem 46.8	GOP +0.4	GOP 46.3/Dem 51.2	Dem +4.9
Georgia	GOP 47.2/Dem 46.8	GOP +0.4	GOP 48.5/Dem 49.4	Dem +0.9
New Hampshire	GOP 47.3/Dem 48.7	Dem +1.4	GOP 44.4/Dem 53.5	Dem +9.1
North Carolina	GOP 51/Dem 44.8	GOP +6.2	GOP 50.5/Dem 47.3	GOP +3.2
Wisconsin	GOP 50.2/Dem 46.6	GOP +3.6	GOP 50.4/Dem 49.4	GOP +1.0
Ohio	GOP 51.8/Dem 43.8	GOP +8.0	GOP 53.2/Dem 46.7	GOP +6.5
Colorado	GOP 44.3/Dem 50.0	Dem +5.7	GOP 41.3/Dem 55.9	Dem +14.6
Washington	GOP 46.3/Dem 49.3	Dem +3.0	GOP 42.6/Dem 57.1	Dem +14.5
Florida	GOP 52.4/Dem 43.6	GOP +8.8	GOP 57.7/Dem 41.3	GOP +16.4

Cheerleaders and Misleaders in 2022

Some of the 2022 averages are stunningly off the mark from the election outcome. One factor could be the absence of Donald Trump on the ballot. But on closer scrutiny there appear to be other problems with the polling averages. The first issue is that the averages include polls taken in the last days (or even on the last day) combined with those taken one and even two weeks earlier. Polls in elections are time sensitive, and even if the pollster is a good one, it is neither correct nor fair to mix polls taken over a period of time or long before the election. As you can see from the RCP charts above, this issue turned out to be more of a problem in 2022 than 2020.

The second challenge, as we can see in the data, is that out of eleven very competitive state races, Democratic candidates were underrepresented in the RCP results in ten cases. To be honest, some averages were off by just a few points, but others missed the mark by nine to eleven points. In each case, the averages were skewed by the presence of Republican pollsters, who were way off in their results in most instances. As I was following the 2022 polls throughout the campaign, and especially in the final weeks, it appeared that any time a Democrat had any kind of momentum, one (or a combination of three) Republican-leaning pollsters would produce results that were *much more favorable to the GOP* and skew the average back to a GOP lead or something more competitive.

I cannot validate motives (if any) behind this situation, but I will strongly suggest that the impact was clear. I did a considerable amount of television over the last month and up to the last day of the campaign, and I was amazed at the bold posturing of the GOP pollsters, who continued to predict a giant "red wave." While it is understood that, as partisan pollsters, their job is to spin for their clients, the overhyping for the party produced expectations that were difficult to match in reality. It was enough, I felt, to raise questions about their public polling results from then on. I am also curious why the aggregator sites allowed these overt partisans to be included in their averages in the first place. On the one hand, I suppose it can be legitimate to include partisan polls with the understanding that polls from both sides of the aisle will balance each other. On the other hand, in 2022, some GOP firms, as I noted above, were much more aggressive in using their polls in a timely way to neutralize any Democratic bounces and in overt spinning to dominate the debate.

The third problem is that the aggregators have taken an inexact science and concluded that by averaging polls and throwing in still-secret algorithms, they can turn compilations of inexact numbers into accurate predictions. In doing so, they unrealistically raise the bar for themselves and for polling in general, and subsequently they create expectations to match. 538 established its reputation in 2008 by getting it right in forty-nine out of fifty states. But "getting it right" meant calling the winner in each state. When pundits define pollsters "getting it right" in the narrowest terms as nailing the actual results to the percent, what good is it to hold the aggregators to a different standard? They are praised for just picking the winners, no matter how close their percentages were. I have learned something that I told the International Association of Political Consultants in London in 2022, just after the November election. An audience member asked me what was in my crystal ball for 2024, and I had the line of the conference when I replied, "I deal in balls of brass, not crystal."

The fourth problem is that on Election Day, the aggregators who have posted the odds of winning every day for months now actually *change* the odds by the hour and then by the minute as the election results start to come in. These postings by 538 and the *New York Times* begin to look like the national-debt ticker on Times Square. They reduce the product down to silliness. In 2022, it became more and more clear that partisan Republican pollsters were working overtime to create a false narrative to bolster a red wave by publishing more frequent polls than were published by more objective established independent pollsters like the universities and newspapers. In Washington State, they reported that longtime US Senator Patty Murray was in trouble in her race against conservative Tiffany Smiley, when Murray actually won by fifteen points. In Wisconsin, to list only one other state, Republican polls were showing that US Senator Ron Johnson was running away with a solid victory over Lieutenant Governor Mandela Barnes, while independent pollsters were showing a very close race, down to the wire. It was, as we could see earlier, a one-point race![4] And those misleading numbers were enough for the Democratic Senate Campaign Committee and Democratic National Committee to withhold much-needed campaign financing from Barnes.

Over the years I have been labeled a Democratic, Republican, or independent pollster. That prompted the former president of my alma mater, Le Moyne College, to introduce me several times as someone who must be doing his job right. Truth is, I am a registered Democrat, and I still screen my information as someone who grew up as a Democrat—but I have done a lot of work for Republican candidates and parties, and for interest groups from different sides, over the years. However, I am also not a formal member of anything, which makes me independent, too. It has likewise allowed me to word my questions in a way that is sensitive to the values and feelings of all sides. So I am tempered in my thinking and have tried to avoid spinning for candidates or commentating on anything but what my polls show. Obviously, there are plenty of partisan pollsters out there, and some are very good ones. But I don't believe they should have ready-made access to television commentating gigs posing as analysts.

There was also a case of "false momentum" polling in 2022. I appeared on several broadcasts with GOP pollsters (for example, Jim McLaughlin on Newsmax) who simply boasted that their party's candidates would win in all the battlegrounds, plus places where no one expected them to do well.[5] I was stunned at the braggadocio without any data to back it up, especially coming from fellow pollsters. I was equally taken aback by their efforts to create expectations that ran the risk of embarrassing them and the party. In addition to raising performance expectations for their clients to dangerous levels, they poorly represented the interests of both their clients and the viewing public. American voters who watch television do not need preachers to the choir; they need the truth. At the same time, it was pathetic watching how Democratic consultants and leaders had started to buy into the GOP narrative of all-out victory and began the process of throwing in the towel. With two weeks to go, unnamed Democratic sources began the blame game for their "losses." As it turned out, not only were the braggarts wrong, but so were the Democratic consultants who were trying to cover their own behinds. Independent voters truly won the day, and they chose their own most important issues and their own dominant values and candidates.

The Ultimate Limits of Polling Aggregation

I had a political science professor in my sophomore year in college who was very nice but heavily reliant on the numbers. I am talking about 1968, and her dominance of the one mainframe computer on campus, plus the punch card heaps found in the garbage bins outside the computer room. I recall that we had two essay exams, an oral presentation, and a term paper to complete. She graded, not surprisingly, on facts, style, validity of argument, and so on, offering a number grade based on each segment of each assignment. We would compare grades on the midterms and speeches—scores like 93.2 percent or 74.6 percent, along with occasional failure of 64.3 percent, with 65 percent being a passing grade. She fed the individual segment ratings into the mainframe, which simply added up her subjective evaluations. These were mainly personal impressions that simply could not be considered totally objective numbers. Then, of course, the mainframe further tabulated the individual grades and (once again using addition and division!!!) came up with a final grade.

Just because it looks like an algorithm, feels like science, makes noise like a signal, and suggests that it's "real clear," does not necessarily mean that it is any of the above. By the way, I got a B in that course—somewhere in the range of 86.3 percent. Although, in retrospect, I should have disputed the grade, because I believed that I should have gotten at least 87.1–87.3 percent. I am just kidding, of course, but who is kidding whom? That grade made me smarter than someone who got 79.4 percent and a loser to a fellow second-year student who might have gotten 89.4 percent (but still only a B). It occurs to me today that our prof could have either thrown the final exams down the stairs and produced the same letter grades or just relied on her fingers and toes. In other words, let's neither pretend nor be pretentious.

Lessons from Chapter 6

What made this effort by GOP pollsters in 2022 extremely pernicious was that these bogus polls were factored in with all the rest on RCP and 538, without disclaimers or commentary. Because these sites were publishing more and more polls by partisans and the independent pollsters were publishing fewer, the GOP pollsters dominated the narrative on Fox, MSNBC, and CNN. And cable news, radio talk, and social media blew up the headlines of a red wave.

But the collaboration of the aggregators in this hoax, trading their reputations for "accuracy," drove the pundits, the conversation, and the public away from a more honest assessment. Pollsters are not perfect, and we should not be put in a position in which missing a race or two means we cannot be counted on. This just should not be our job. Again and again, we are polling human beings. What I have outlined in New Jersey about a substantial percentage of voters making up their minds or actually changing their minds at the last minute is very real. My job as a pollster is to capture the trend line and be able to explain it in a reasonable way. My job is not to be mixed in with those who have their own partisan agendas.

The aggregator websites overall do a good job, but they are in the same category with Cassandra and Prometheus as accurate forecasters of the future. For all the reasons noted so far, no one can really do that. (Truly, the ancient god and prophetess were not so oracular themselves!!!) And with a further bow to the ancients, my concern is that we let these sites become the modern-era Icarus, who flew on his wax wings too close to the sun.

New York Mets manager of the 1986 World Champions Davey Johnson was the pioneer in using a computer with a statistics package in the dugout. He was controversial at the time and misunderstood by even his own star players. The Mets won in 1986. But sometimes the ideal batter for the key moment in the ninth inning would strike out. We can be very good at what we do, and use the odds based on analytics to improve our chances of success, but hardly ever can we be perfect. Essentially, no matter how good the program, the algorithms, the training, the staff, and the gifted minds in leadership, algorithms still cannot erase human error, subjectivity, and fate.

So, what should we make of all of this fascination with aggregation, forecasting, and hubris? We can begin by using accurate terminology for each profession. One who creates, conducts, and analyzes his/her own work in polling is indeed a "pollster." One who reads, evaluates, creates scoring for polls, and makes leaps into the world of prediction by forecasting is not a pollster, just as one who reads mystery novels and plays a mean game of *Clue* is not a detective. We can go a long way in presenting honesty to the public and to our own clientele by being honest with ourselves. There is plenty of room for all of us in this business, but let's recognize that there are limits to numbers and perhaps even more limits to piling numbers on numbers.

CHAPTER 7

The Ones That Got Away

The very funny and wicked comedian Joan Rivers used to say, before an especially juicy and nasty piece of gossip, "Can we talk?" I was actually on her show a couple of times, so this chapter is a paean to Joan, albeit a pain for me.

The laws of probability most often in political polling operate on a 95 percent confidence rate—that is, if we do the same random survey the same way one hundred times, we should get the same results plus or minus the margin of error in ninety-five cases out of one hundred. Thus, there can always be those nasty 5 percenters that just do not work. We all know that. Everyone in this field does, but my colleagues/rivals were always watching me very closely. Even though I paid attention to and learned a lot from some less-than-accurate results, in the words of the 1965 megahit by British pop singer Sandie Shaw, "There is always something there to remind me."

Polling relies very heavily on good statistical data, but as I have already said, there is some artwork involved as well. Our work is not (and cannot be) dominated by the bots of artificial intelligence. This chapter is dedicated to the genius of Pablo Picasso, who, amid his numerous masterpieces, produced *The Young Girl with a Flower Basket*, ranked by many among the worst paintings of all time.[1] I am no Picasso, but I have had a few masterpieces in my life. This chapter is not about them and ideally illustrates what can go wrong.

My Home State (1998 and 2000)

As background, New York is the original "What's in it for me?" state, as I learned way back in political science class and in pounding the pavement during campaigns for many years. Based from the beginning on a mercantile economy,

New York evolved into an individualistic culture. New Yorkers always wanted government action on behalf of both business and the public. We'll never cut taxes and we'll always overspend because people want it both ways. In my lifetime, New Yorkers have only sent two conservatives to the United States Senate: James Buckley in 1972 and Alfonse D'Amato in 1980. Both, however, were beneficiaries of three-way races in which the liberal vote was split. D'Amato built a reputation as "Senator Pothole," more our local councilman than an international figure like Daniel Patrick Moynihan or Jacob Javits.[2]

There are plenty of stories about Senator D'Amato's intervention and spectacular results on behalf of constituents with smaller problems. And he was legendary in terms of bringing home the bacon—that is, federal largesse—to his home state. He was especially popular in previously forgotten parts of upstate New York. In 1998, he had become chairman of the powerful Appropriations Committee, which meant that he would no longer have to stand in line for New York's share of bacon. He actually held the knife that was cutting the pork. So how did he lose his bid for reelection in 1998? All he needed to do was flout his power and ability to bring home more for New York! Instead, his pollster and strategist decided to go on automatic pilot and attack opponent Chuck Schumer as a "liberal."[3]

In 1998, I blew my first big-time race, in New York State, of all places. In designing my turnout model, I assumed I needed a larger representation of Republicans. I had many reasons for this assumption at the time. The state's Republican governor, George Pataki, was very popular, and 1998 polls showed that progressive Democrats, always a key factor in New York politics, were not terribly pleased with the moderate dealmaker, Congressman Chuck Schumer. In all 1994 races, Republicans swept every statewide office because of large upstate New York and Republican turnouts. I assumed that New York City would play a smaller role, as it did in both 1990 and 1994, and that many Democrats would stay home. I built my sample around New York City, representing 29 percent of votes cast in the Senate race.

Table 7.1. NY Post/Fox 5 News/Zogby Poll, November 1, 1998
MOE +/- 3.2 Percentage Points

	Region							
	Total		Upstate		Suburbs		NYC	
	f	%	f	%	f	%	f	%
D'Amato	519	50.5	270	63.0	156	54.4	93	29.7
Schumer	509	49.5	158	37.0	131	45.6	220	70.3
Total	1029	100.0	428	100.0	288	100.0	313	100.0

	Race							
	Wt Non-Hisp		Hispanic		Afr Amer		Other/Mix	
	f	%	f	%	f	%	f	%
D'Amato	451	55.3	26	46.8	18	18.5	17	43.2
Schumer	365	44.7	30	53.2	81	81.5	22	56.8
Total	815	100.0	56	100.0	99	100.0	39	100.0

	Religion								Gender			
	Catholic		Protestant		Jewish		Other/ None		Male		Female	
	f	%	f	%	f	%	f	%	f	%	f	%
D'Amato	272	61.9	161	54.8	22	18.2	58	37.4	278	53.6	241	47.3
Schumer	167	38.1	133	45.2	98	81.8	97	62.6	241	46.4	269	52.7
Total	439	100.0	295	100.0	120	100.0	155	100.0	519	100.0	510	100.0

	Political Party							
	Total		Democrat		Republican		Indep/Other	
	f	%	f	%	f	%	f	%
D'Amato	519	50.5	117	25.7	311	81.8	92	47.0
Schumer	509	49.5	337	74.3	69	18.2	103	53.0
Total	1029	100.0	454	100.0	380	100.0	195	100.0

	Income											
	< $15,000		$15–24,999		$25–34,999		$35–49,999		$50–74,999		$75,000+	
	f	%	f	%	f	%	f	%	f	%	f	%
D'Amato	41	44.4	68	54.7	59	49.2	88	55.6	98	54.2	93	47.9
Schumer	51	55.6	56	45.3	61	50.8	70	44.4	83	45.8	102	52.1
Total	93	100.0	125	100.0	120	100.0	158	100.0	180	100.0	195	100.0

	Age							
	18–29		30–49		50–64		65+	
	f	%	f	%	f	%	f	%
D'Amato	75	52.9	172	51.7	134	49.7	137	49.3
Schumer	67	47.1	161	48.3	136	50.3	141	50.7
Total	141	100.0	333	100.0	270	100.0	279	100.0

It actually was 31 percent in 1998—only a two-point difference, except that Schumer mopped up there and it gave him a bigger edge. At the same time, I felt that D'Amato was popular enough in upstate and New York's suburbs. I was wrong. It turns out that I conflated turnout models from previous gubernatorial races, in which Democrats suffered from lower voting rates (1990 and 1994), with relatively higher turnouts in federal elections in the state. There is no question in my mind that there was a lack of enthusiasm among many Democrats for Schumer. But that's not the point here. I was wrong.

Then I followed up with the same miscalculation in the 2000 Senate race of First Lady Hillary Clinton against Long Island Republican Congressman Rick Lazio. In both 1998 and 2000, I had two tight races down to the wire. None of my competition got the full extent of the Democratic victories, but I was stuck at two nearly tied races. Schumer won by ten points, Clinton by twelve.

Table 7.2.   NY Post/Fox 5 News/Zogby Poll, November 1, 2000 MOE +/– 4.0 Percentage Points (set 1 of 3)

	Total		Region					
			Upstate		Suburbs		NYC	
	f	%	f	%	f	%	f	%
Clinton	347	50.8	121	44.5	83	41.8	144	67.3
Lazio	328	48.1	149	54.8	112	56.8	67	31.3
Dunau	6	.8			3	1.4	3	1.4
Other	2	.3	2	.6				
Total	683	100.0	272	100.0	198	100.0	213	100.0

	Party					
	Democrat		Republican		Independent	
	f	%	f	%	f	%
Clinton	247	81.0	43	17.9	57	41.5
Lazio	57	18.8	196	81.3	75	54.9
Dunau	1	.2	2	.8	3	2.3
Other					2	1.3
Total	305	100.0	241	100.0	137	100.0

	Age Group							
	18–29		30–49		50–64		65+	
	f	%	f	%	f	%	f	%
Clinton	57	57.9	99	49.1	91	51.2	89	49.3
Lazio	35	36.1	102	50.4	86	48.4	91	50.7
Dunau	4	4.2	1	.5	1	.4		
Other	2	1.8						
Total	98	100.0	202	100.0	178	100.0	180	100.0

**Table 7.2.   NY Post/Fox 5 News/Zogby Poll, November 1, 2000
MOE +/- 4.0 Percentage Points (set 2 of 3)**

	Age Group-B									
	18–24		25–34		35–54		55–69		70+	
	f	%	f	%	f	%	f	%	f	%
Clinton	26	55.1	60	56.4	111	48.3	75	50.6	65	50.4
Lazio	15	32.2	46	43.6	117	51.0	73	49.4	64	49.6
Dunau	4	8.9			2	.7				
Other	2	3.8								
Total	47	100.0	106	100.0	230	100.0	147	100.0	129	100.0

	Race									
	White		Hisp		Afr Amer		Asian		Other	
	f	%	f	%	f	%	f	%	f	%
Clinton	227	42.5	36	88.4	66	92.1			13	62.1
Lazio	302	56.5	5	11.6	6	7.9	7	100.0	6	27.3
Dunau	4	.7							2	10.6
Other	2	.3								
Total	535	100.0	40	100.0	71	100.0	7	100.0	20	100.0

	Union				Under17			
	Yes		No/NS		Yes		No/NS	
	f	%	f	%	f	%	f	%
Clinton	129	59.4	217	46.8	103	50.7	244	50.9
Lazio	87	40.3	240	51.7	96	47.5	232	48.3
Dunau	1	.3	5	1.1	4	1.9	2	.4
Other			2	.4			2	.4
Total	217	100.0	464	100.0	203	100.0	480	100.0

	Total		Religion					
			Catholic		Protestant		Jewish	
	f	%	f	%	f	%	f	%
Clinton	347	50.8	123	41.6	91	47.6	46	58.0
Lazio	328	48.1	170	57.5	98	51.3	33	42.0
Dunau	6	.8	3	.9	2	1.0		
Other	2	.3						
Total	683	100.0	297	100.0	191	100.0	80	100.0

Table 7.2. NY Post/Fox 5 News/Zogby Poll, November 1, 2000 MOE +/- 4.0 Percentage Points (set 3 of 3)

	Religion				Born Again			
	Muslim		Other		Yes		No/NS	
	f	%	f	%	f	%	f	%
Clinton	2	65.5	79	75.5	26	41.3	65	50.8
Lazio	1	34.5	23	21.9	37	58.7	61	47.7
Dunau			1	.9			2	1.5
Other			2	1.7				
Total	3	100.0	105	100.0	63	100.0	128	100.0

	Status									
	Married		Single		D/W/S		Together		NS	
	f	%	f	%	f	%	f	%	f	%
Clinton	187	47.7	66	57.6	76	50.6	16	74.0	3	49.2
Lazio	200	51.3	45	39.1	74	49.4	5	26.0	3	50.8
Dunau	4	1.0	2	1.7						
Other			2	1.5						
Total	391	100.0	114	100.0	151	100.0	21	100.0	6	100.0

	Gender				Outside			
	Male		Female		Yes		No/NS	
	f	%	f	%	f	%	f	%
Clinton	150	45.8	197	55.5	102	60.2	95	51.3
Lazio	173	52.7	156	43.8	65	38.1	90	48.7
Dunau	3	.9	3	.8	3	1.7		
Other	2	.5						
Total	327	100.0	356	100.0	170	100.0	185	100.0

	Income											
	< $15,000		$15– 24,999		$25– 34,999		$35– 49,999		$50– 74,999		$75,000+	
	f	%	f	%	f	%	f	%	f	%	f	%
Clinton	27	49.6	52	65.9	39	53.9	49	49.1	56	46.2	74	51.9
Lazio	28	50.4	27	34.1	31	43.3	50	50.9	62	51.5	69	48.1
Dunau					2	2.8			1	.8		
Other									2	1.5		
Total	55	100.0	79	100.0	72	100.0	99	100.0	121	100.0	143	100.0

As I looked at these for the first time in more than two decades, I really didn't do so badly after all. Quinnipiac University in Connecticut nailed the margin, and I congratulate them, but I feel there could have been a late surge for Clinton. Other pollsters were closer to my results. In scrutinizing these pages, I see where I might have fallen down a bit with New York's regions. My sample had 39.8 percent from upstate, 28.9 percent from New York City's suburbs, and 31.1 percent from New York City. Actual election results revealed that 37.7 percent came from upstate, 29.7 percent from the suburbs, and 32.6 percent from New York City. So, for this book, I reweighted my results by region and still came up with a Clinton margin of 51 percent to 48 percent against Lazio.

Clinton was running all over New York State. She was doing everything right, which would not be true later in her 2016 presidential bid. She went on a "listening tour" in almost every corner of the state and won people over by actually doing that, listening, and also staying until the last person got to visit with her and it was past time to turn out the lights.[4] She marched in the July 4 parade in Lowville, New York, a good six hours from Fifth Avenue. And her opponent, Rick Lazio, was a solid guy, but no match for an icon who really worked hard. Truth is, he spent too much time on the campaign bus and not enough with the people. But I still had a close race.

Alan Elsner of Reuters offered one possible explanation for my not getting the right margin at the end in the Clinton/Lazio race. He felt it could have been the introduction used by my telephone interviewers, who would open by saying they were doing a poll for the "*New York Post* and Zogby International." Perhaps, Elsner suggested, they provided a slight bias toward the GOP candidates? But I had the very same close race in 2000 for the Albany newspaper, which had no history of conservative bias. Our interviewers were instructed to open with "Hi, my name is ____ and I am doing a brief poll for the *Albany Times Union*." For my part, I do believe that I overrepresented Republican voters in those samples, but I also know that both Senate races were indeed close until movement toward Schumer and Clinton at the end. One other poll had Schumer in the lead by four points going into Election Day 1998. The same was true of Clinton's smaller lead in 2000. But my performance was simply not that good—especially after so much success over the years in New York and elsewhere. In my case, it became clear: I had again oversampled upstate New York and Republican voters, because I was perhaps overcorrecting for what I analyzed as undersampling by my competitors. As I noted in chapter 1, that formula had worked before.

All of us in this business ultimately have to base our results on a turnout model. This is what we feel that the actual electorate will look like on Election Day.[5] Some of us simply go with the exit polls from the most recent similar race and adjust our current samples to reflect that history. Others look at demographic trends—for example, do we expect more Blacks or Hispanics to turn out than last time? Still others examine the news and measure whether there is any reason that one side or the other has voters with less enthusiasm, which may lead to fewer of a key group coming out to vote. I use all three, and that is as much artwork as it is science. I am, after all, a historian, and I have a history of using soft data, too.

While still on the subject of New York State, this reminds me of two totally unrelated but funny (I think) stories. They represent for me a kind of unique grounding I experience located in an older, ethnic, working-class, unpretentious city. One involves a local election in one of the Utica Common Council districts in the late 1990s. A friend of mine, Pat Y., was running again for a seat he had once held. His lawn signs were simple: "Who Cares? Pat Y. Cares." It appears that a small group of neighborhood kids decided to have fun one night and whited out the bottom half of the signs all over the district, so they just read, "Who Cares?"

Just a few years ago, a neighboring town held an election for town highway superintendent, a very important position. One candidate ran as an independent, and his lawn signs read, "Vote for_____. Absolutely No Experience." Y. won; the independent lost. While pundits bloviate about issues of great concern to Americans, be mindful that there are thousands (probably millions) who are not paying close attention or who don't really care—and yet may still vote.

2004: Good Polling, Wrong Analysis, or, It All Boiled Down to Ohio

The race for the presidency in 2004 was a close one. In my daily tracking for Reuters, the lead between George W. Bush and John Kerry would seesaw over the last six weeks. The interesting thing is that Kerry barely ever moved from 48 percent. It was Bush whose numbers would fluctuate. There were loyal Republicans who were disappointed in Bush. Some were deficit hawks who helplessly watched the national debt trajectory. Others were libertarian and First Amendment devotees troubled by the Patriot Act. And finally, there were opponents of the war in Iraq. They were still Republicans, but at times they would park in the "undecided" parking lot.

The polling numbers on a daily level followed a similar pattern to the razor-thin race in 2000, when Al Gore had won the popular vote only to be eclipsed by a single vote in the Electoral College and then a single vote in the United States Supreme Court. As in 2000, Florida was a key battleground, but the most important bellwether and ultimate determinant of victory was Ohio, with its twenty electoral votes in 2004. With the lead changing several times, the race entered the final phase with both candidates just about tied at 48 percent.[6] At the same time, we were doing daily tracking for Reuters in eight states, and there were no clear clues on a winner in any of them right up to the closing bell.

In the third week of October, as we continued our daily tracking nationally and in the states for Reuters, Knight-Ridder Newspapers commissioned us to conduct a wide-ranging online poll of the culture and identity of voters. Perhaps my most famous question to come out of that poll was "Which candidate would you most want to have a beer with?" Although Bush didn't drink because he had been a recovering alcoholic for decades, he was still the winner in a landslide.[7] As in other polls, Kerry led on nine of ten issues, including the economy, health care, education, and other domestic matters, ceding only national security to Bush. However, Bush's lead on handling this issue was 64 percent to 24 percent—a significant deficit for Kerry during the wars in Afghanistan and Iraq. Generally, Republicans do score better on matters of national security, and Bush, while his numbers were declining, was still seen as leading the war on terror.[8]

Knight-Ridder Newspapers wanted us to do focus groups in key battleground states among undecided voters only. I personally did four of the group discussions, while senior staff did two. We chose key cities in swing states: Dearborn, Michigan; Wilkes-Barre, Pennsylvania; Cleveland, Ohio; St. Paul, Minnesota; and Orlando, Florida. We developed the scripts over the duration due to dynamics and events in the campaign, using key insights from the earlier groups. Focus groups are not science and are not meant to be. And, as I noted in the introduction, I don't like to come into focus group discussions with long scripts, but I do have some questions to generate conversation. For example, I want to know what motto governs their lives, who they trust most when it comes to key decisions that affect their lives, whether they mainly stick to one party or vote for the candidate who impresses them most, and what they aspire to be. Do they have any heroes, and if so, who and why? I want to get into their heads and hearts. I use raised hands or scores to measure progress. But the keys to successful focus groups involve interpersonal dynamics, creative play, strong and weak personalities, the ability of one person to persuade, and the possibilities for consensus. I want to know how they respond to situations, their thought processes, and what is most important to them in making their decisions.

These swing-state folks, about twelve to fifteen in each city, likely had voting histories but were now truly undecided in 2004. The first two groups were like watching paint dry. That is an occupational hazard with focus groups, but fortunately a rare one. In a 1987 Syracuse diocese focus group in Binghamton, New York, there is actually video of me looking at my watch every few seconds. Fact is that focus groups are not as easy as they may appear. Recruitment is not automatic. We have to offer financial incentives to get people to come, and a few may still not show up. We must send reminders as well as pay for gas and parking. We also need to screen to be sure we get the demographic and political mix we are looking for. There is always the risk that a babysitter doesn't show up or another family commitment gets in the way. Finally, anything can happen when total strangers meet for the first time. Is the chemistry right? Will there be one blowhard? Or will we get a very shy person who is not accustomed to speaking in groups?

But these 2004 battleground focus groups were fascinating and lively, except that as of the third week in October, they still had no idea who they were going to vote for. Even worse, neither did I after meeting them. And for those who cannot believe that people have not chosen their candidate by mid-October, remember that good citizenship is a luxury to many people, who are struggling to keep a family together, get the kids to school on time, or find the energy to pay attention when they are working multiple jobs.

Overall, they reinforced that Kerry was better on the so-called soft issues: health care, education, the environment, Social Security. However, as in the surveys for both Knight-Ridder and Reuters, Bush got higher marks for handling terrorism and national security. Far and away, these undecided voters in every city preferred to have a beer with Bush over Kerry.[9] This was for the most part a key barometric reading, because, as I look back over the years in my lifetime, it has been clear that the more affable candidate has won the presidency—such as Harry Truman over the dour Thomas Dewey. "I Like Ike" Dwight Eisenhower over the effete Adlai Stevenson. The electric John F. Kennedy over the shadowy Richard Nixon. A beer with rowdy and bawdy Lyndon Johnson over the ideological Barry Goldwater? Of course. And so on through Reagan, George H. W. Bush, Bill Clinton, Barack Obama, and Donald Trump. The only exception I have seen was 1968, when the Happy Warrior Hubert Humphrey lost a race to Richard Nixon, albeit a new and improved—"Tanned, Rested, and Ready," as his consultants spun—Nixon. But Humphrey was probably the guy to down a couple of brews with. Nixon was the better guy to join you in a late afternoon whine with a "red, red wine." (By the way, another legend is that the taller candidate normally wins. Kerry's six-foot, four-inch frame alone should have sent him to the White House.)[10]

The focus group respondents in every city said they paid no attention to negative political commercials (folks always say that), but when I asked them the first thing that came to mind when they heard the name John Kerry, they repeated verbatim, "I was for it before I was against it." This statement referenced a frequently running negative commercial about his first voting to appropriate eighty-seven billion dollars to fight the wars in Afghanistan and Iraq and then voting against it. Even though he never said those exact words, they were used in the ad to show that he flipped on issues and, in a crisis, would be indecisive. The participants also knew quite a lot about Kerry going windsurfing during the Labor Day holiday—something meant to show that this elitist was just not regular folks.

In the last two cities—St. Paul and Cleveland—I tried something different. I showed them portraits of Abraham Lincoln, Franklin D. Roosevelt, John F. Kennedy, and Ronald Reagan. All participants were able to identify the former presidents, and most were able to give me the most positive traits they saw in each. Lincoln was seen as "decisive," "courageous," "tough with his adversaries," "compassionate." Roosevelt was identified with "caring for the common man," "triumphing over adversity," "rallying the nation in tough times," "likable." Kennedy represented "optimism," "vision," and "youthful change." And Reagan was "an average guy," "always positive," "strong and decisive," "inspirational," "standing up to adversaries," and "cheerful." That was about as much as I could get from them.

I thought it would be a good idea to then show portraits of the two candidates and see which of the attributes from the four iconic presidents they could identify with the two men seeking the post. The answer? Nothing. Absolutely nothing. That was the ultimate clue for me, that moment of clarity. Despite any or no information that each person in the focus groups may have had, they just could not pin down one factor that could help them decide. Thus, they really didn't know who they were going to vote for, just like I didn't know who was going to win. Sure, they'd rather have a beer with George W. Bush, but he was no Jack Kennedy or Harry Truman, and yes, John Kerry could get high marks on handling important domestic issues, but they just couldn't get their arms around him.

Focus groups are always valuable, because we get to really and truly talk to people, especially, in this case, those who honestly had no idea who they would vote for. In some instances, there was angst: "I know I have to vote, but I just don't like either one." In other cases, there was confusion: "I wish I could merge Kerry's intelligence with Bush's nice-guy image." Clearly no one saw what they were looking for, and most didn't even know what it was. Bush's senior adviser Karl Rove turned an old campaign maxim on its head. Instead of finding the opponent's weaknesses and turning the screws, he would find the opponent's strengths and turn them into negatives. Hence, Kerry's valiant service in Vietnam was depicted as narcissistic, self-serving, and even fraudulent. He would no longer be seen as the war veteran opposed by a good-time-loving draft dodger. And Bush, who had been untouchable as the president who was leading the nation in a war against terrorism, would be depicted as a failure in life and a puppet in the hands of his own vice president and secretary of defense. The participants were well aware of all of this. But I could never replace the sense of seeing and hearing it for myself. That is something that a checkmark on a survey and a mere data point on a spreadsheet cannot express.

Soon after the focus groups, I went on *The Daily Show* with Jon Stewart. He is privately a very thoughtful and serious man—for example, in the greenroom chatting before the show. But on the show, he was a whole lot of fun, with no script and notes. After warming up the live studio audience, he asked me which candidate was going to win. I probably should have said that I really didn't know, but I felt that the audience wanted a key to what I was thinking, so I said with conviction, "Kerry." I had been saying that Kerry would probably win since May

2004, with the caveat that Bush would most likely not be able to improve his numbers. But I was on Comedy Central's top program, not at a seminar held by the Center for Strategic and International Studies or Harvard's John F. Kennedy School of Government. I was on a show having fun, and I was supposed to tell the audience who I thought would win. Truth is that Bush really did not improve his numbers. He went into Election Day with a 46 percent approval rating, and only 45 percent felt he deserved reelection. I lost a lot of friends on the right after that Comedy Central appearance, but I spoke what I believed. The race promised to be as close as the one in 2000, and predicting how it would turn out was risky business. By the way, Jon Stewart called me every day after that for the latest numbers. After the election, I realized how much people counted on me, almost as a soothsayer, and I knew that sort of image had a very short shelf life.

Table 7.3.   Reuters/Zogby International, November 2, 2004 (set 1 of 5)

| | Party Recoded | | | | | | | |
| | Total | | Democratic | | Republican | | Independent | |
	f	%	f	%	f	%	f	%
Bush	481	49.4	41	10.9	316	91.3	123	49.4
Kerry	478	49.1	332	87.8	26	7.5	121	48.3
Nader	7	.7	5	1.3	1	.3	1	.5
Badnarik	1	.1					1	.4
Peroutka	3	.3			1	.3	2	.8
Cobb								
Other	3	.4			2	.5	2	.6
Undecided								
Total	974	100.0	378	100.0	346	100.0	250	100.0

| | Age Group | | | | | | | |
| | 18–29 | | 30–49 | | 50–64 | | 65+ | |
	f	%	f	%	f	%	f	%
Bush	59	33.6	229	54.9	116	50.4	74	52.0
Kerry	114	65.2	180	43.1	111	48.4	67	47.1
Nader	2	1.2	2	.4	2	.8	1	.9
Badnarik					1	.4		
Peroutka			3	.7				
Cobb								
Other			3	.8				
Undecided								
Total	175	100.0	416	100.0	229	100.0	142	100.0

Table 7.3. Reuters/Zogby International, November 2, 2004 (set 2 of 5)

	Investor Class				Armed Forces			
	Yes		No/NS		Yes		No/NS	
	f	%	f	%	f	%	f	%
Bush	165	54.4	310	46.9	110	53.4	369	48.2
Kerry	133	43.9	342	51.7	94	46.0	383	50.0
Nader	3	.9	4	.7	1	.6	6	.8
Badnarik	1	.3					1	.1
Peroutka			3	.4			3	.4
Cobb								
Other	2	.5	2	.3			3	.5
Undecided								
Total	304	100.0	661	100.0	205	100.0	765	100.0

	Religion Recoded									
	Total		Catholic		Protestant		Jewish		Other/None	
	f	%	f	%	f	%	f	%	f	%
Bush	479	49.7	134	50.5	259	58.1	7	23.7	80	35.6
Kerry	470	48.8	128	48.2	177	39.7	23	76.3	143	63.8
Nader	7	.7	2	.6	5	1.1			0	.1
Badnarik	1	.1							1	.4
Peroutka	3	.3			3	.7				
Cobb										
Other	3	.4	2	.6	2	.4				
Undecided										
Total	964	100.0	265	100.0	446	100.0	30	100.0	224	100.0

	Born Again			
	Yes		No/NS	
	f	%	f	%
Bush	158	61.7	100	52.9
Kerry	91	35.5	86	45.7
Nader	4	1.7	1	.3
Badnarik				
Peroutka	1	.4	2	1.1
Cobb				
Other	2	.7		
Undecided				
Total	256	100.0	189	100.0

Table 7.3. Reuters/Zogby International, November 2, 2004 (set 3 of 5)

	Income											
	< $15K		$15–25K		$25–35K		$35–50K		$50–75K		$75K+	
	f	%	f	%	f	%	f	%	f	%	f	%
Bush	22	32.8	31	36.5	44	43.8	62	47.6	96	46.9	165	60.6
Kerry	46	66.7	51	59.6	56	55.0	68	52.4	102	49.9	105	38.6
Nader	0	.5	2	2.7	1	1.2			3	1.3	1	.2
Badnarik			1	1.2								
Peroutka									2	1.0		
Cobb												
Other									2	.9	2	.6
Undecided												
Total	68	100.0	86	100.0	101	100.0	130	100.0	205	100.0	273	100.0

	Age Group-B											
	Total		18–24		25–34		35–54		55–69		70+	
	f	%	f	%	f	%	f	%	f	%	f	%
Bush	477	49.5	31	33.1	72	42.9	220	53.7	107	54.5	47	49.1
Kerry	472	49.0	63	66.9	92	54.7	181	44.3	88	44.7	48	50.1
Nader	7	.7			2	1.3	4	.9	1	.3	1	.9
Badnarik	1	.1							1	.5		
Peroutka	3	.3			2	1.2	1	.2				
Cobb												
Other	3	.4					3	.8				
Undecided												
Total	963	100.0	94	100.0	168	100.0	409	100.0	196	100.0	95	100.0

	Race										Union			
	White		Hisp		AfrAmer		Asian		Other		Yes		No/NS	
	f	%	f	%	f	%	f	%	f	%	f	%	f	%
Bush	428	56.5	29	39.2	12	12.7	5	53.1	6	18.9	96	41.9	384	51.9
Kerry	320	42.3	45	60.8	82	86.7	5	46.9	20	68.9	132	57.4	343	46.4
Nader	7	.9			1	.5							7	1.0
Badnarik	1	.1											1	.1
Peroutka									2	6.8			3	.4

Table 7.3.   Reuters/Zogby International, November 2, 2004 (set 4 of 5)

	Race									Union			
	White		Hisp		AfrAmer		Asian		Other		Yes		No/NS	
	f	%	f	%	f	%	f	%	f	%	f	%	f	%
Cobb														
Other	2	.2							2	5.4	2	.7	2	.2
Undecided														
Total	757	100.0	74	100.0	94	100.0	10	100.0	30	100.0	230	100.0	740	100.0

	Live											
	Total		Lge City		Sm City		Suburbs		Rural		NS	
	f	%	f	%	f	%	f	%	f	%	f	%
Bush	481	49.4	107	35.2	134	53.2	102	52.5	135	62.8	3	35.2
Kerry	478	49.1	194	63.9	111	44.2	90	46.1	78	36.0	5	64.8
Nader	7	.7			3	1.4	1	.6	2	1.1		
Badnarik	1	.1			1	.4						
Peroutka	3	.3	1	.3	2	.8						
Cobb												
Other	3	.4	2	.6			2	.8				
Undecided												
Total	973	100.0	304	100.0	251	100.0	195	100.0	216	100.0	8	100.0

	Ideology												
	Prog		Lib		Mod		Cons		VCons		Libert		NS	
	f	%	f	%	f	%	f	%	f	%	f	%	f	%
Bush	22	25.9	22	12.7	108	37.0	250	82.9	50	84.4	11	64.4	17	37.7
Kerry	62	72.2	148	87.3	179	61.4	45	15.0	8	14.0	5	30.0	29	62.3
Nader					4	1.5	3	.9						
Badnarik											1	5.6		
Peroutka							2	.7	1	1.6				
Cobb														
Other	2	1.9					2	.6						
Undecided														
Total	86	100.0	170	100.0	291	100.0	301	100.0	59	100.0	18	100.0	46	100.0

Table 7.3. Reuters/Zogby International, November 2, 2004 (set 5 of 5)

| | Gender | | | | | |
| | Total | | Male | | Female | |
	f	%	f	%	f	%
Bush	481	49.4	239	50.7	242	48.1
Kerry	478	49.1	224	47.5	255	50.7
Nader	7	.7	3	.7	4	.7
Badnarik	1	.1	1	.2		
Peroutka	3	.3	2	.4	1	.2
Cobb						
Other	3	.4	2	.4	2	.3
Undecided						
Total	974	100.0	470	100.0	503	100.0

| | NASCAR fan | | | | Passport | | | |
| | Yes | | No/NS | | Yes | | No/NS | |
	f	%	f	%	f	%	f	%
Bush	128	58.0	349	46.6	172	43.6	306	53.3
Kerry	89	40.3	389	51.9	214	54.1	262	45.8
Nader	4	1.7	3	.4	6	1.4	1	.3
Badnarik			1	.1			1	.2
Peroutka			3	.5	2	.4	2	.3
Cobb								
Other			3	.5	2	.4	2	.3
Undecided								
Total	221	100.0	749	100.0	395	100.0	573	100.0

Table 7.4. Zogby International Online Poll, November 2, 2004 (set 1 of 4)

	Party									
	Total		Democratic		Republican		Independent		Libertarian	
	f	%	f	%	f	%	f	%	f	%
Bush	21818	49.2	1567	9.1	14667	94.6	5504	48.7	81	36.4
Kerry	21494	48.5	15560	90.1	666	4.3	5246	46.4	21	9.6
Nader	222	.5	63	.4	12	.1	146	1.3	1	.5
Badnarik	338	.8	24	.1	73	.5	122	1.1	118	53.1
Peroutka	179	.4	1	.0	42	.3	135	1.2	1	.4
Cobb	49	.1	7	.0	1	.0	41	.4		
Other	61	.1	28	.2	10	.1	23	.2		
NS	147	.3	27	.2	40	.3	79	.7	0	.1
Total	44308	100.0	17279	100.0	15511	100.0	11297	100.0	222	100.0

	Age Group C							
	18–29		30–44		45–59		60+	
	f	%	f	%	f	%	f	%
Bush	2925	36.8	6479	50.4	7006	49.1	5325	58.6
Kerry	4693	59.0	6052	47.1	7053	49.4	3640	40.1
Nader	70	.9	67	.5	57	.4	27	.3
Badnarik	136	1.7	109	.8	70	.5	22	.2
Peroutka	59	.7	58	.5	34	.2	28	.3
Cobb	19	.2	11	.1	16	.1	4	.0
Other	16	.2	27	.2	13	.1	5	.1
NS	33	.4	44	.3	34	.2	34	.4
Total	7951	100.0	12847	100.0	14282	100.0	9085	100.0

	Religion							
	Catholic		Protestant		Jewish		Other/None	
	f	%	f	%	f	%	f	%
Bush	6541	53.8	12036	60.3	268	20.6	2584	25.9
Kerry	5429	44.7	7526	37.7	1015	77.9	7069	70.8
Nader	33	.3	85	.4	7	.6	80	.8
Badnarik	53	.4	110	.6	7	.6	153	1.5
Peroutka	38	.3	115	.6	1	.0	22	.2
Cobb	2	.0	13	.1	1	.1	31	.3
Other	25	.2	15	.1	1	.1	21	.2
NS	35	.3	74	.4	2	.2	29	.3
Total	12157	100.0	19973	100.0	1303	100.0	9988	100.0

Table 7.4. Zogby International Online Poll, November 2, 2004 (set 2 of 4)

	Age Group									
	Total		18–29		30–49		50–64		65+	
	f	%	f	%	f	%	f	%	f	%
Bush	21735	49.2	2925	36.8	9581	50.5	5287	49.9	3941	59.5
Kerry	21438	48.5	4693	59.0	9006	47.4	5141	48.5	2598	39.2
Nader	221	.5	70	.9	89	.5	41	.4	20	.3
Badnarik	337	.8	136	1.7	141	.7	46	.4	14	.2
Peroutka	178	.4	59	.7	72	.4	26	.2	21	.3
Cobb	49	.1	19	.2	17	.1	12	.1	1	.0
Other	61	.1	16	.2	32	.2	10	.1	3	.0
NS	145	.3	33	.4	52	.3	34	.3	25	.4
Total	44163	100.0	7951	100.0	18991	100.0	10598	100.0	6623	100.0

	Income											
	< $15K		$15–25K		$25–35K		$35–50K		$50–75K		$75K	
	f	%	f	%	f	%	f	%	f	%	f	%
Bush	425	31.8	965	42.8	1709	44.6	2999	50.5	5097	51.8	8153	48.1
Kerry	806	60.2	1197	53.2	2034	53.1	2819	47.7	4546	46.2	8540	50.4
Nader	9	.7	46	2.1	28	.7	32	.5	40	.4	44	.3
Badnarik	34	2.5	19	.8	29	.8	42	.7	64	.7	104	.6
Peroutka	37	2.8	9	.4	13	.3	16	.3	36	.4	42	.2
Cobb	12	.9	6	.3	7	.2	9	.1	7	.1	7	.0
Other	3	.3	7	.3	3	.1	0	.0	22	.2	13	.1
NS	10	.8	2	.1	12	.3	27	.5	21	.2	53	.3
Total	1338	100.0	2251	100.0	3834	100.0	5944	100.0	9833	100.0	16956	100.0

	Children<17			
	Yes		No/NS	
	f	%	f	%
Bush	7961	58.5	13762	45.0
Kerry	5381	39.6	16081	52.6
Nader	44	.3	178	.6
Badnarik	80	.6	254	.8
Peroutka	69	.5	108	.4
Cobb	15	.1	35	.1
Other	13	.1	49	.2
NS	34	.3	110	.4
Total	13597	100.0	30576	100.0

Table 7.4. Zogby International Online Poll, November 2, 2004 (set 3 of 4)

| | Gender | | | | | |
| | Total | | Male | | Female | |
	f	%	f	%	f	%
Bush	21659	49.2	11360	53.7	10299	45.0
Kerry	21400	48.6	9152	43.3	12247	53.5
Nader	216	.5	102	.5	114	.5
Badnarik	335	.8	275	1.3	61	.3
Peroutka	177	.4	133	.6	44	.2
Cobb	49	.1	33	.2	16	.1
Other	61	.1	25	.1	37	.2
NS	147	.3	59	.3	87	.4
Total	44044	100.0	21139	100.0	22905	100.0

| | Education | | | | | | | |
| | <HS | | HS Grad | | Some Col | | Col+ | |
	f	%	f	%	f	%	f	%
Bush	115	59.6	1851	66.7	7080	54.8	12722	44.9
Kerry	71	36.9	850	30.6	5526	42.7	12015	53.0
Nader	1	.3	34	1.2	53	.4	135	.5
Badnarik	2	.9	18	.7	130	1.0	187	.7
Peroutka			9	.3	71	.5	99	.3
Cobb	5	2.4	3	.1	11	.1	31	.1
Other			4	.1	19	.1	37	.1
NS			8	.3	42	.3	95	.3
Total	193	100.0	2777	100.0	12932	100.0	28322	100.0

| | Race | | | | | | | | | |
| | White | | Hisp | | Afr Amer | | Asian | | Other | |
	f	%	f	%	f	%	f	%	f	%
Bush	17328	51.4	1709	49.5	1256	29.0	147	34.0	670	51.6
Kerry	15721	46.6	1647	47.7	2970	68.7	276	63.8	550	42.4
Nader	106	.3	26	.7	49	1.1	4	.9	29	2.2
Badnarik	259	.8	16	.4	25	.6	1	.1	14	1.1
Peroutka	112	.3	40	1.2	6	.1			12	.9
Cobb	31	.1	6	.2			0	.1	8	.6
Other	38	.1	2	.0	17	.4			2	.1
NS	111	.3	10	.3			5	1.1	13	1.0
Total	33710	100.0	3456	100.0	4322	100.0	432	100.0	1297	100.0

Table 7.4. Zogby International Online Poll, November 2, 2004 (set 4 of 4)

	Live											
	Total		Lge City		Sm City		Suburbs		Rural		NS	
	f	%	f	%	f	%	f	%	f	%	f	%
Bush	21743	49.2	6939	41.9	4927	52.3	5539	50.6	4313	59.9	25	40.9
Kerry	21460	48.6	9237	55.8	4267	45.3	5182	47.3	2739	38.0	36	58.4
Nader	222	.5	94	.6	65	.7	37	.3	26	.4		
Badnarik	337	.8	142	.9	76	.8	76	.7	44	.6	0	.6
Peroutka	178	.4	65	.4	30	.3	39	.4	45	.6		
Cobb	49	.1	26	.2	11	.1	6	.1	7	.1		
Other	61	.1	17	.1	16	.2	20	.2	8	.1		
NS	146	.3	36	.2	29	.3	56	.5	24	.3		
Total	44198	100.0	16555	100.0	9421	100.0	10955	100.0	7206	100.0	61	100.0

	Status										
	Married		Single		D/W/S		Together		NS		
	f	%	f	%	f	%	f	%	f	%	
Bush	16331	58.1	2673	30.5	2361	43.5	300	17.9	9	26.3	
Kerry	11228	40.0	5750	65.7	2979	54.9	1354	80.6	24	71.8	
Nader	103	.4	79	.9	27	.5	5	.3	1	1.8	
Badnarik	160	.6	141	1.6	22	.4	10	.6	0	.2	
Peroutka	126	.4	34	.4	15	.3	1	.1			
Cobb	15	.1	21	.2	6	.1	7	.4			
Other	38	.1	18	.2	2	.0	3	.2			
NS	93	.3	42	.5	12	.2					
Total	28094	100.0	8757	100.0	5425	100.0	1680	100.0	33	100.0	

	Union			
	Yes		No/NS	
	f	%	f	%
Bush	3855	45.3	17897	50.1
Kerry	4424	52.0	17037	47.7
Nader	70	.8	151	.4
Badnarik	52	.6	283	.8
Peroutka	39	.5	139	.4
Cobb	15	.2	34	.1
Other	25	.3	36	.1
NS	20	.2	125	.4
Total	8501	100.0	35703	100.0

This was a close one, and both of my nationwide polls—one by my in-house call center, the other online—were showing close to the very same thing. For the most part, key demographic subgroups were aligned, with the major exceptions being among Blacks and Hispanics, as the above data shows. While the online polling was not ready for prime time in several states, it was pretty impressive nationally.

Election Day 2004 was weird again for me. The Susquehanna International Group near Philadelphia, a global investment trading fund, asked me to poll nationwide and in key states, just as I had in 2000, the weekend before *that* election. They wanted to be able to run to the market with the "sure winner" before any of their competitors and could not wait for the first tranche of exit polls, which would be released around 1:00 p.m. They needed results by 11:00 a.m. or noon at the latest. We conducted our daily tracking on a 3:00 p.m. to 3:00 p.m. cycle. Up until then, we were capturing four hundred new respondents each day between those hours, folding the new sample into the previous two days of samples (four hundred and four hundred) and creating a new rolling average sample of twelve hundred likely voters each day. With the investment firm's support, we were able to add an additional one thousand voters on each of the last three days in order to get a very large and even more accurate new sample to capture any late trends.

The problem is that when we stopped polling, just before 11:00 a.m. EST on Election Day, we still had no clear vector and, for that matter, no clear victor. I called the investment firm and told them to give me another hour. One hundred more telephone calls later, the race was still too close to determine. This situation was very disappointing to me, because we were paid handsomely back in 2000, and I couldn't make an indisputable call for the winner back then either. Now here we were again, with a sizable deposit in our account, and we still could not point to the victor. We stayed on the phones, and our final result nationwide was Bush 49.8 percent to Kerry 48.4 percent. While Kerry was staying at that flatline 48 percent, Bush's approval and "the reelect" numbers, as we call them in the polling business, were just not good. Besides, we now had Kerry up in Ohio by a few points. At the same time, the always (previously, anyway!) early exit polls were coming out discreetly, and they were showing Kerry with a seven-point lead in Ohio, a double-digit lead in Pennsylvania, and a lead in Virginia.

I got on the phone with the leaders of the Philadelphia firm and said it was too close, but I thought we were looking at a Kerry victory.

"Are you sure?"

"Of course not."

They again, as in 2000, told me I needed to make a call, a prediction. Since I couldn't in 2000, I decided I just had to do something this time. I called it for Kerry.

I closely examined both my telephone and online polling, and the latter results were similar enough to the exit polls in those three states. I decided to post those results by late afternoon with a Kerry victory prediction. By five o'clock I was again, as in 2000, at the Foreign Press Center in DC, explaining why I was calling the election for Kerry. When I was done and comfortably in a taxi heading back from the National Press Building to our office on 16th and K, I played thirteen piled-up phone messages. Eleven were members of the press leaving congratulations for calling another victory correctly. One was from a DC correspondent for the *New York Daily News* who was with the Bush family and inner circle, who reported that they seemed resigned to a defeat.

The last was at 8:15 p.m. from my wife, telling me that it was looking like a Bush victory.

What happened?

It all boiled down to Ohio, which turned around after 5:00 p.m. It was also about very troubled exit polling that year, as in 2000. We used to be able to "go to the bank" with the 1:00 p.m. results. As we later learned, thanks to early voting trends and some problematic exit polling, these could no longer be relied on.[11] And the final factor is that I bowed to pressure to make a call. Too bad, because my polling 49.8 percent Bush to 48.4 percent Kerry was very close to 50.8 percent Bush to 48.4 percent Kerry. And my online national poll showed Bush leading 50 percent to 48.4 percent—even closer. I should have just stayed with what I said in the first place: "Too close to call." Despite having nailed the national popular vote once again, I was empowered by the early network exit polls to go one step further and be ahead of the curve. Since the early exit polls were very similar to my online polls showing a distinct Kerry advantage, I was emboldened to go one step too far. As it all turned out, the exit polls were way off, and so was my prediction.

About ten days before that election, I had flown from Anchorage, where I had given a speech to the Western Region meeting of the Council of State Governments, to Miami to do press before and after the second presidential debate between Senator Kerry and President Bush. I sat in business class next to a young man who told me he was truly undecided on who to vote for. After we talked a bit, I made a fake gun with my fingers and I kiddingly said, "You have five seconds to decide." He told me he just couldn't say, so I gave him my card and told him to call me when he made his decision. (He was actually the sky marshal, and I am a little embarrassed at my gesture.) One of the calls after my Election Day phone messages from the Foreign Press Center was from that sky marshal, who told me that, after a lot of soul searching, he decided to cast his vote for Kerry. And I thought I was riding high again. Until the last voicemail message, which I mentioned above was from my wife. And there went my day and evening.

Bush won Ohio, and it was the second time that a disputed large state would put him over the top. (Remember, of course, Florida in 2000.) The right-wing *National Review* declared that I was finished, and Peggy Noonan, the former speechwriter for President Ronald Reagan, called my Election Day numbers "bizarro." But both the *New York Post* and the *Boston Globe* called me among "the big winners" of the day. Both of my national polls—online and telephone—were fine, but online I clearly fell down in some states, especially Arkansas and Colorado. In Arkansas, we simply did not have enough well-distributed samples to draw from, and our targeted telephone calling to Black voters was insufficient. It was a powerful learning experience for all of us about ensuring that before we do any polling in a small state or a city, we have enough usable emails. As for Colorado, I have generally had a problem with that state, including my telephone surveys. Perhaps it is the rapidly changing demographics, which include young people, a steady influx of Latinos, conservatives, and liberals. That is not an excuse. It is merely an observation that this is one state that has been unusually troublesome for me.

In retrospect, it is still difficult for me to see how President Bush could have won with a 45 percent approval rating and less than 40 percent saying the country was headed in the right direction. I received a call from lawyer and activist Robert F. Kennedy Jr., who did a brilliant piece about how the Republicans "stole" the election for *Rolling Stone*.[12] I also visited with iconoclastic author Christopher Hitchens, who wanted to take a trip to Ohio to find out what happened. I told them I will always feel there was something fishy but that I had no evidence at all. And we have to have evidence. Or at least we used to.

Debut of the Controversial Zogby Interactive Poll

This is perhaps the optimum time to get into the most famous and controversial topic of my political polling—the Zogby Interactive Polls, conducted online. I have already outlined the standard methodology for surveys and a few points—party weighting and listed phone numbers—in which I veered away from industry standards in the 1980s and 1990s. The use of telephone landlines was becoming increasingly problematic. For those pollsters automatically funded by huge endowments and network news budgets, it was possible to continue with live calls and not worry about interviewer fatigue and spiraling costs. I had seen the handwriting on the wall right after the 1996 elections. Telephone response rates were plummeting, and internet usage and email communications were growing exponentially. I wrote a piece for the journal *Public*

Opinion in 1997 saying that internet political polling was coming soon, and the following year Zogby Interactive began research and development. The process we used in those early days to build our internet panel was tortuous but necessary. We created links with other websites by directly asking whether we could; we also used a typical late 1990s method of bartering banner ads with those sites in exchange for a question on a national telephone survey. It helped enormously that Rush Limbaugh and other radio commentators were talking about us and that early MSNBC and Fox and other lesser-known cable television news constantly interviewed me.

I remember my assistant coming in and saying that Rush Limbaugh was on the phone. I had just come out with the first Reuters/Zogby Poll showing the Clinton/Dole race at only a six-point Clinton advantage in June 1996. I picked up the phone.

"Mr. Zogby? This is Rush Limbaugh. I have a radio program."

I responded that, uh, I knew that. However, "Before we get started, I want you to know that I am a liberal."

"So that means your polls are honest. I like that."

I tell this story to make clear that I didn't champion Republican causes but that I saw what was coming. Two articles came out after that, one in the *Washington Times* and one for Reuters, claiming I had a right-wing agenda. This was never true. I never gave conservatives or liberals what they wanted. I gave them the numbers and analysis they needed. We were also doing plenty of telephone polling for major daily newspapers and local television stations nationwide, as well as for regular client work, so we were able to develop a list of about one hundred thousand emails in short order, which was impressive for the time.

We also asked people who responded to our telephone surveys whether they wished to be included in our online surveys. Regularly around 20 percent of each sample obliged, and we already had collected their demographics. We started using our call center to validate their personal information. By 2004, we had about five hundred thousand distinct emails when we were contacted by the editor of the *Wall Street Journal Online*. They wanted to produce what was then technologically advanced, a twice-weekly, full-color map of all fifty states and where the presidential race stood in each state. This image would appear on the splash page of the website, and they wanted us to supply the polling numbers. I got back to him within twenty-four hours with an appropriate seven-figure price for polling and collecting the polls of others. He came back and offered an unsuitable low-five-figure price. But how do I turn down the *Wall Street Journal* and its full-color, half-page, cobranded coverage twice a week? So I regrouped with my team and figured out a way to make it work. Polling the larger and midsize states online would be no problem. We could draw decent-sized and well-distributed (i.e., regionally and demographically representative) samples. In some of the smaller states we would have to supplement with telephone calls. We would have to do the same in those areas where there were higher nonwhite concentrations, and also areas—then quite abundant, and mainly but not always rural—still trailing behind with their internet access.

In several states we had the problem of demographic distribution, an over-representation of Republicans (remember, a lot of our earlier panel members had joined because of Rush Limbaugh!), so we would have to get pretty creative with weighting. We, of course, were doing lots of statewide polling in battleground and a few nonbattleground states and would lead with those. But we ran the online polling exercise in as many states as we could. One clear limitation is that our final tracking polls had to begin a whole week before Election Day in order to get target sample sizes. Thus it was more difficult to get the best last-minute changes, because things could shift over the final days of a campaign. Nonetheless, in addition to our daily tracking by telephone for Reuters, we were filling a novel type of map for the *Wall Street Journal Online.*

On Election Day 2004, our *national* online poll was near perfect: George W. Bush 50.8 percent to John Kerry's 48.8 percent. The real score was 50.4 percent to 48.4 percent. Altogether we got sixteen of twenty states we were regularly polling online correct. Some of the margins were off a bit, but we got the winners and where this happened, and our numbers were actually similar to the exit polls. The experience and experiment were worth the *Wall Street Journal Online's* discount to us. Only Harris Interactive was doing online political polling besides us—although they used only a national sample, no states—and both we and Harris were far ahead of the curve. Why wasn't Harris Interactive doing what we were doing? Well, in 2004 this whole thing of polling online was that new, and I might not have done it so soon if the *Wall Street Journal Online* hadn't asked.

This leads me to a challenge. I polled the nation and battleground states for Reuters and C-SPAN in 2008. On my own, I unleashed our online sample and polled the nation and twenty states simultaneously. I was happier with the results, because our sample had grown and had better representation of key demographics. But I was also running a very busy business, so I was forced to halt the online polling on October 4, 2008, because I needed the sample for client work and just didn't have the capacity to be sending emails out every day to tens of thousands of people.

When our last results were published in early October, they were right in the mainstream of other polling at the time. But this was the moment when the polling aggregators entered the limelight, with their averaging of polls and creation of algorithms to magically "predict" outcomes. They used my early October results to stand for my final election results and outcomes. That was one-dimensional and perhaps even a willful misuse of polling data to make me look bad. For that reason, and because these aggregators change their predictions daily (then hourly on election days), I have not always found them useful, or at times even honorable, although in some instances elsewhere in this book I do defend them.

New Hampshire and California Primaries (2008)

In 2008, there were a few mistakes that stand out, and I need to explain them as much as I had to own them back then. These were all live telephone polls. In the first instance, I was polling the pivotal New Hampshire primary featuring senators Barack Obama (who had just won the Iowa caucuses), John Edwards (who had come in second in Iowa), and Hillary Clinton (the third-place finisher). My polling had been spot on again in Iowa, because I have a whole history there. Normally, the winner of Iowa receives a big bounce going into New Hampshire, and 2008 would be no exception. Obama's lead over his two opponents jumped to as high as twelve points in New Hampshire. But 2008 was different. In the past, there had been at least a two-to-three-week spread from Iowa to New Hampshire, so there was time for an initial bounce to settle down or at least take shape. That year, however, the caucuses fell on a Thursday night, and New Hampshire voters went to the polls the following Tuesday. A mere six days. In other words, it would be difficult to project that Obama's bounce after Iowa would dissipate in such a short time.

From Thursday to Saturday, the Illinois senator's lead jumped to twelve points over the former First Lady. On Sunday, now doing a two-day (not three-day) rolling average, Obama's lead stayed at twelve points. Saturday night, ABC held a debate. Clinton's two male opponents ganged up on her—but that had no impact on the Sunday numbers. On Monday she appeared on ABC's *Good Morning America* speaking with a small group of middle-aged New Hampshire women, being wistful about a woman possibly not winning the Oval Office. She actually got teary-eyed.[13] Those who were polled Monday morning and early afternoon were not moved by her at all. Indeed, it was too early for a Monday morning event to wind its way through public opinion within just twenty-four hours. But after 5:00 p.m. the night before the primary, Clinton jumped to a five-point lead among the 124 voters actually polled between 5:00 p.m. and 9:00 p.m. What's a pollster to do? The late Monday sample was not large enough to stand alone, so I had to factor in Sunday's and earlier Monday's output and still showed Obama with a twelve-point lead. At the end of my release, I indicated that we saw possibly some late-breaking movement toward Clinton. But I had to hedge.

The Clinton numbers on Monday night turned out to be a real surge that continued into Tuesday, the day folks in New Hampshire actually voted. Of course, Clinton won the primary and pollsters looked bad. Gallup and Zogby shared the worst results, each showing a twelve-percentage-point lead for

Obama. It really was not a moment of pride for any of us. I was again invited on the *Daily Show* with Jon Stewart, and he asked me what happened.[14] I started to explain and then stopped abruptly simply because it was too long for television, it would sound defensive, and a comedy show was just not the best forum. Instead, I just swallowed. Then I said, "Wow, Gallup really sucked." I got severely criticized by the American Association for Public Opinion Research (AAPOR) for not defending myself, but it was comedy in front of a live audience, so no, I don't have any regrets about just passing the buck.

Two weeks later was Super Tuesday, and I did have a super one—that is, except for California. Because it *was* California, I was standing on tectonic plates. I want to say right off the bat here, and right on the page, that I blew it. I mean really messed up! But there was actually more to it than that. It reminds me of the sign my brother saw a woman holding up at the Democratic National Convention in 1984: "Don't Blame Me. I Ain't Never Been Here Before!" An unprecedented, nonpartisan primary in California was just completely new turf; thus we had no past polling to offer as a guide. No idea what the ultimate turnout model might look like. We were honestly staring into an abyss.

As I told the chief political reporter for the *Los Angeles Times*, "I was in a fetal position for twenty-four hours after the primary." I was really walking upright, but also humiliated, especially since I was polling for both Reuters and C-SPAN. Hillary Clinton defeated Barack Obama by ten points. I had the ten-point spread correct—except that I had Obama leading.[15] I channeled my inner Shirelles ("Mama said there'd be days like this") and proceeded to have an internal team do a thorough audit. I had been not only wrong but also wrong before the entire world. The problem was that we drew a bad sample. California was using for the first time an open primary in which anyone could vote, so there was no historical trend to rely on. Translated, that meant that we had no guide from previous primaries on a turnout model: What region do they typically come from? What is the distribution of a "typical" turnout by age, gender, race, city/suburban/rural, and so on? We were flying blind, but we decided to plunge in nonetheless.

We found that we grossly oversampled young Latino voters, when the exit poll showed that they did not come out in great numbers. Older Latinos did vote, and chose Hillary Clinton, but they were underrepresented in our sample. That was enough right there. Pollsters aim for a 95 percent confidence rate, and this was among the 5 percent! Congratulations to the late robo-poll pioneer Jay Leve of SurveyUSA, who nailed that one.[16] I have no idea why he got it right, but he did.

By the way, I asked a very bright intern from the University of Pennsylvania in our DC office to lead our internal audit, going back to study previous polling in which we were right on the money. She reported two possibilities: one, that we just drew a bad sample, or, she wondered, could I have been just lucky the dozens of other times? (We did have a going-away party for her, but we waited until two weeks after she left to celebrate!)

The other pollsters did not even dare touch California, and I don't know for sure why (fatigue? budget? recognition that it wouldn't work?). But I was fearless. I had done Iran, and later Albania, so thought I had this. A month later, I was on a panel sponsored by the Advertising Research Foundation in New York with Gail Collins of the *New York Times* and Obama's chief pollster Joel Benenson.

Someone yelled out, "What happened in California?"

"I fucked up."

Enough said.

Lessons from Chapter 7

Sometimes the black swans, those unaccounted for and unexpected results, come with soot all over them. Remember, in survey research involving random probability rules, our best "confidence rates" are 95 percent. That means there still are those unwanted and uncalled-for moments when things just go wrong. Unfortunately, I save that 5 percent for the highest-visibility times when the whole world is watching. I have learned to hedge a little bit since.

There is a famous scene in the Scottish play (I don't want to curse my own book) when Lady Macbeth gives a long soliloquy on guilt for her role in a brutal murder she has prodded her husband to commit. Then comes a knock at the gate. It brings her back to reality, along with the reader (audience). There is nothing like a knock at the gate when you are wrong with a huge audience.

Nothing like it at all. Especially in front of an audience of millions of people. Damn.

When you go out on a limb, especially exposing yourself professionally to tens of thousands (or even millions) of people, there is no turning back. When a *New York Times* correspondent rang me a few days later and asked how I felt after the Kerry call, I told him I was embarrassed but happy that no one was hurt emotionally or physically by my prediction. Others did not see it that way and thought my response was snarky! Which—I guess—it was. But I learned to not make predictions anymore. Just suggestions. What we must not forget, however, is that the polling was actually quite good.

I saw Senator Kerry two years later when I was invited to brief the Senate Democrats on issues in the 2006 elections, and I apologized for the mess-up.

"I still don't think you were wrong," he said.

Maybe I wasn't after all, but perhaps I was reckless.

In any event, a real moment of clarity came from none other than a long-time CBS and NBC foreign correspondent, Marvin Kalb. He responded to a public apology I had posted on the Zogby International website for my mistaken "prediction" of the Kerry victory in 2004. In his email he said, "Just forget about it." He and others respected the quality of my analysis, not the pinpoint accuracy of every prediction. Just stick with it, he said.

Public polling is always a high-risk challenge, but it offers high rewards if you can do it, because it can establish a record of your accuracy and credibility—two very appealing credits to marketers, communicators, CEOs, human resources professionals, lobbyists, not-for-profits, and strategists/consultants. Even missing an election by a few points is still good enough. Think about it this way: In most other client work, we are not calling an election, but something else entirely. If 51 percent of your consumers or 42 percent of your employees take a position on something, it is not really necessary to have the lowest margin of error. The meaning is pretty clear to allow for planning or marketing.

We all want to be loved, but public polling leaves those of us who practice it wide open to criticism. It doesn't actually hurt business if you are attacked, but if your skin is thin, then you need to just get a grip on it and take it. I have always operated by the LARGAS Rule—"Like Anyone Really Gives a Shit." So, I get one wrong. People will forget if you just let them.

Warning: If your line of work involves guarding the nuclear "football" for the president and you accidentally set off a nuclear war, then ignore this chapter. Otherwise, who really cares about your (and my) mistakes and the criticism received? Does NBA superstar Steph Curry explain missing a possible game-winning shot, or does a couple stop making love midstream because "Zogby said Schumer was tied, and he actually won by double digits"?

My son and business partner, Jeremy, lived in Prague for two years and was teaching history at one of their local colleges. On one of our visits, he was anxious for me to meet his department head. We ran into this fellow at a large shopping mall, and he was stinking drunk at two o'clock in the afternoon.

"Did you see what was said about me?" he asked even before exchanging an opening salutation.

Of course, I hadn't.

He proceeded to show a two-inch letter to an obscure journal critiquing a short paper he had written. He was outraged.

My only thought was: LARGAS! And I couldn't have been the only one to not care.

The point is simple: we all make mistakes. Those who are small enough to point them out or dwell on them are the ones with the real problem. Not many people truly have the fortitude to drop it and just go on.

So how do I handle insults? Well, I have a lot of experience. There are some options. The first is simply to ignore them, which is the least satisfying. Second is to insult right back, which is very satisfying but not a productive use of your or my time.

And the third? Write a book.

Despite the critics of polling in general and mine specifically, our work can be quite rewarding, and all we have to do is keep our eyes on the prize. In polling elections, the publicity you receive, plus being able to establish a record of accuracy, can go a long way toward building your brand. It creates a much greater level of awareness of who you are and information in the public domain that you can discuss and write about.

In 2006, the Center for Strategic and International Studies (CSIS) invited me to serve as a commissioner on Smart Power, a study group formed to beef up US public diplomacy efforts. At the very first meeting in Washington, I walked into a small conference room and saw Harvard's Joseph Nye, the foremost expert on the use of "smart power"; Richard Armitage, former undersecretary of state under Colin Powell; former Supreme Court justice Sandra Day O'Connor; and a number of leading (if not iconic) figures in the foreign policy establishment. I felt like one of those SAT questions (or a Muppets song) that asks, "One of these things is not like the other?"

When it came time to do a short self-introduction, I noted how honored I was to be in their presence and to serve with such an august group. Dr. Nye interrupted me and said, "But, John, you are the one who has real data. We don't bring that." I had not thought about it that way. Sometimes, it isn't who you are; it's what you've got.

I still recall fondly that in 2000 one of the earlier email recipients who regularly opened our daily tracking polls was a person in Vatican City. I wonder whether it was His Holiness.

These mistakes have led me to greater introspection about what being a pollster is really about. We are not the pope, high priests, sorcerers, oracles, or gods. We are just people in a profession that generates good data and provides useful and important interpretations of it. But just like the heart surgeon who loses a patient or a police officer who trips while chasing a suspect, our careers are not over and our profession is not dead because of a mistake. We pollsters have to learn that we don't make war and peace, and we don't generate any more carbon dioxide than anyone else. We are like meteorologists, economists, and other professional prognosticators. We do make mistakes. But the fate of humankind generally does not hang in the balance. Hopefully we are better for it, and the world is no worse because of it.

And there's an important point to keep in mind. Many of those who get the most airtime to bloviate about us actually cannot read or understand what our numbers may be really saying! We get less airtime.

As for the ones that got away, I refer back to the words of songwriters Kelly Gordon and Dean Kay via Frank Sinatra: "I just pick myself up and get back in the race. That's life." For me, that has meant a measure of both anticipation and responsiveness. In 1998, as we prepared for our annual strategic planning meeting, now with sixty to seventy people, we hung up signs that read "The Smartest Pollster." We had traded well off our record of accuracy, but that simply could not last forever. We needed to rebrand ourselves as the pollsters located in small-town middle America who were able to capture what we used in another tagline, "What people all over the world are really thinking," because that is truly what we were and still are. And we pushed aggressively forward with our online polling, believing correctly that the telephone would increasingly lose its relevance as a research tool and because online polling could offer our clients and ourselves much more data.

In both instances, I believe, we remained ahead of the curve.

CHAPTER 8

The Perils of Polling Overseas Elections

I call this the *Star Trek* chapter—that is, "To boldly go where no man has gone before." Polling can be done almost everywhere. We can begin by taking North Korea out of the picture, but we have done work in eighty countries, including ones that on the surface appear to be impossible. For example, we asked political questions in the Kingdom of Saudi Arabia, did elections in Iran, and polled on levels of support for terrorist groups like al-Qaeda in Muslim countries from Indonesia to Morocco. I never tried polling Syria, and by far the most difficult one has been Egypt. Prior to 2011, we did ask about political issues, except we dared not ask people to rate the job performance of President Hosni Mubarak. I suppose we could have tried, maybe once! And a number of places, including Egypt, have since eased up because of our use of mobile technology, rather than our folks risking their well-being by asking questions in public places.

In the old days, we had to rely on hiring students and independent contractors to conduct face-to-face interviews, which would take weeks to complete. These days we have been enabled by less expensive technologies like email, text messages, and text-to-web polling. The results are accurate, but the significant takeaway for me has been using the art of asking about values and using metaphorical questions to get at the heart and soul of what people are really thinking.

Iran (2001)

One of my favorite global stories occurred in May 2001. I was in Paris, hosted by an Italian fixer who set up a meeting for me and a colleague with two government officials from Russia. We were exploring possible polling opportunities in the Kremlin. (Yes, that Kremlin!) I received a call from my brother, who was sitting with the then minister of information for the UAE in Abu Dhabi. The sheikh at the time was heading Abu Dhabi Television, for whom Jim produced and hosted a show on US politics for many years. Sheikh Abdullah bin Zayed wondered whether we could poll the upcoming June presidential election in Iran. Incumbent president Mohammad Khatami, a reformer often at odds with the ayatollahs, was running for a second term. The neighboring UAE wanted to see whether the Iranians still had an appetite for reforms. It was also hoping to make history by being a foreign country commissioning a poll in Iran.

I immediately called my good friend in Mexico City, who had served as the president of the World Association for Public Opinion Research (WAPOR), of which I was a member. I asked whether he knew of any possible resources in Iran who could be mobilized in short order to conduct the polling fieldwork. He gave me the name of an Iranian national who was a professor, then located at the Maxwell School of Citizenship and Public Affairs at Syracuse University. Coincidentally, I had done my master's and doctoral studies at Maxwell, just down the road from Utica. I immediately called this professor from Paris, and he teamed me up with two professors from the University of Tehran. Within forty-eight hours, our team was on the field.

The most important takeaway from this whole event is much more than the global story of our rapid turnaround. It is even more than the fact that we nailed the election. Not having the luxury of time and staff to poll the entire country, we focused on the seven major cities with over one million in population and their suburbs. These included places like Tehran, Mashhad, Isfahan, Karaj, Tabriz, Shiraz, and Qom—as well as a random sample of cities/suburbs throughout the country. Rural areas were expected to vote overwhelmingly conservative and generally ignore politics and ideology in favor of bread-and-butter localized issues. We sampled one thousand Iranian adults with face-to-face interviews by students who were paid. In our sample we had President Khatami leading 77 percent to 14 percent over his nearest rival, the ultraconservative Ahmad Tavakkoli. The actual result was his victory by 76.9 percent to 15.58 percent![1] A good couple of days' work, but better than that was the information we were able to glean from the questions we asked.

Of course, we could not pose real political policy questions because we did not want to frighten respondents, such as whether Iranians felt the country was headed in the right direction, how they felt toward the United States, or whether they had favorable views toward Supreme Leader Ayatollah Ali Khamenei. But we did wonder, if they were offered a chance to visit any city from the following list, which would they choose: Paris, Mecca, Dubai, New York, or Singapore? The winner was Paris, showing best that the respondents, who (like the population as a whole) were mainly under thirty years of age, would opt for the West over either Muslim glitz or holy sites. New York came in second.[2] It had been widely reported that during the Iranian Revolution in 1979, which culminated

in the rise to power of the ultraconservative Ayatollah Ruhollah Khomeini, thousands of young people in the streets demanding an end to the brutal pro-US shah
were actually reformers who were just using the old mullah as a lever to get rid of
the ultrarepressive shah and then move on to their own agenda. Young women
were wearing makeup and Jordache jeans under their full-cover burkas, and men
were listening to Western music.[3]

What followed in 1979 was a fundamentalist regime as brutal as that of the
shah, a suppression of all freedoms of expression, mass executions, paranoia, and
repression of women. The ayatollah, much to the marchers' and the rest of the
world's surprise, was not a transitional figure. He lived for another decade and
made sure of a like-minded conservative successor. Two decades after the death
of Khomeini, when tens of thousands of young reform-minded protesters again
hit the streets of Tehran, it was clear that they still opposed the ultraconservative
regime and still carried some Western sympathies.[4] Our poll in 2001 showed
that their views beyond the horizon were again more focused on Western cities
like Paris (30 percent of the sample, 41 percent of those eighteen to twenty-
four years old, none of whom were old enough to even remember the 1979
revolution) and New York—not "death to America," as the followers of the
ayatollahs had been shouting. As we would discover in numerous polls of Iran
and the entire Middle East region, Iranians shared a deep antipathy toward US
policies—but not toward "America," a beacon of freedom. In that 2001 poll,
the most important thing is that we got to do it in the first place, though there
was a tragic story. The University of Tehran professors who led the field team
conducting the fieldwork were also critics of the conservative Islamic regime.
They were subsequently arrested for treason, which carried the death penalty. I
personally had to sign a statement pledging that I was not working for the CIA.
Their sentences were commuted, and then they were released from prison.

**Table 8.1.   Abu Dhabi Television/Zogby Iran Poll, June 4, 2001
MOE +/- 4.5 Percentage Points (set 1 of 6)**

| | Total | | Age Group | | | | | |
| | | | 15–24 | | 25–64 | | 65+ | |
	f	%	f	%	f	%	f	%
Tavakoli, Ahmad	35	10.5	18	16.5	15	7.5	2	9.1
Jasbi, Abdollah	11	3.3	6	5.5	4	2.0	1	4.5
Khatami, Sayyed Mohamadd	249	75.0	75	68.8	156	77.6	18	81.8
Razavi, Sayyed Mansouer	7	2.1	1	.9	6	3.0		
Shamkhani, Ali	6	1.8	1	.9	5	2.5		

Table 8.1. Abu Dhabi Television/Zogby Iran Poll, June 4, 2001
MOE +/- 4.5 Percentage Points (set 2 of 6)

	Total		Age Group					
			15–24		25–64		65+	
	f	%	f	%	f	%	f	%
Sadr, Sayyed Shahabodin	4	1.2	1	.9	3	1.5		
Ghafoorifard, Hasan	7	2.1	4	3.7	2	1.0	1	4.5
Kashani, Sayyed Mahmood	4	1.2	2	1.8	2	1.0		
Hashemitaba, Sayyed Mostafa	1	.3			1	.5		
Non	8	2.4	1	.9	7	3.5		
Total	332	100.0	109	100.0	201	100.0	22	100.0

	Iran Direction									
	Right Direction		Wrong Track		Not Sure		Don't Know		Irrelevant	
	f	%	f	%	f	%	f	%	f	%
Tavakoli, Ahmad	10	7.2	17	15.3	5	14.7	2	7.1	1	4.8
Jasbi, Abdollah	3	2.2	4	3.6	1	2.9	1	3.6	2	9.5
Khatami, Sayyed Mohamadd	112	81.2	75	67.6	27	79.4	20	71.4	15	71.4
Razavi, Sayyed Mansouer	3	2.2	2	1.8			2	7.1		
Shamkhani, Ali	1	.7	3	2.7					2	9.5
Sadr, Sayyed Shahabodin	3	2.2							1	4.8
Ghafoorifard, Hasan	2	1.4	3	2.7			2	7.1		
Kashani, Sayyed Mahmood	1	.7	3	2.7						
Hashemitaba, Sayyed Mostafa	1	.7								
Non	2	1.4	4	3.6	1	2.9	1	3.6		
Total	138	100.0	111	100.0	34	100.0	28	100.0	21	100.0

Numbers should be added with those on the previous page, understanding that because of rounding and weighting, they will not exactly equal 100.

Table 8.1. Abu Dhabi Television/Zogby Iran Poll, June 4, 2001
MOE +/- 4.5 Percentage Points (set 3 of 6)

	Social Position					
	Upper		Middle		Lower	
	f	%	f	%	f	%
Tavakoli, Ahmad	1	1.9	28	12.2	6	12.0
Jasbi, Abdollah	1	1.9	9	3.9	1	2.0
Khatami, Sayyed Mohamadd	49	92.5	162	70.7	38	76.0
Razavi, Sayyed Mansouer			6	2.6	1	2.0
Shamkhani, Ali	1	1.9	4	1.7	1	2.0
Sadr, Sayyed Shahabodin			3	1.3	1	2.0
Ghafoorifard, Hasan			6	2.6	1	2.0
Kashani, Sayyed Mahmood			4	1.7		
Hashemitaba, Sayyed Mostafa			1	.4		
Non	1	1.9	6	2.6	1	2.0
Total	53	100.0	229	100.0	50	100.0

	Single		Gender				Status					
			Female		Male		Single		Married		Else	
	f	%	f	%	f	%	f	%	f	%	f	%
Tavakoli, Ahmad	35	10.5	22	13.5	13	7.7	18	15.1	17	8.3		
Jasbi, Abdollah	11	3.3	7	4.3	4	2.4	5	4.2	5	2.5	1	12.5
Khatami, Sayyed Mohamadd	249	75.0	122	74.8	127	75.1	87	73.1	154	75.5	7	87.5
Razavi, Sayyed Mansouer	7	2.1	4	2.5	3	1.8	1	.8	6	2.9		
Shamkhani, Ali	6	1.8	3	1.8	3	1.8			6	2.9		
Sadr, Sayyed Shahabodin	4	1.2	2	1.2	2	1.2	1	.8	3	1.5		
Ghafoorifard, Hasan	7	2.1	1	.6	6	3.6	4	3.4	3	1.5		
Kashani, Sayyed Mahmood	4	1.2	1	.6	3	1.8	2	1.7	2	1.0		
Hashemitaba, Sayyed Mostafa	1	.3			1	.6			1	.5		
Non	8	2.4	1	.6	7	4.1	1	.8	7	3.4		
Total	332	100.0	163	100.0	169	100.0	119	100.0	204	100.0	8	100.0

Table 8.1. Abu Dhabi Television/Zogby Iran Poll, June 4, 2001
MOE +/- 4.5 Percentage Points (set 4 of 6)

	Education						Ethnicity			
	Low		Middle		High		Fars		Other	
	f	%	f	%	f	%	f	%	f	%
Tavakoli, Ahmad			29	10.6	6	14.3	25	11.1	10	9.6
Jasbi, Abdollah			10	3.7	1	2.4	11	4.9		
Khatami, Sayyed Mohamadd	15	100.0	200	73.3	32	76.2	170	75.2	77	74.0
Razavi, Sayyed Mansouer			7	2.6			2	.9	5	4.8
Shamkhani, Ali			5	1.8	1	2.4	3	1.3	3	2.9
Sadr, Sayyed Shahabodin			4	1.5			2	.9	2	1.9
Ghafoorifard, Hasan			7	2.6			4	1.8	3	2.9
Kashani, Sayyed Mahmood			4	1.5			4	1.8		
Hashemitaba, Sayyed Mostafa			1	.4			1	.4		
Non			6	2.2	2	4.8	4	1.8	4	3.8
Total	15	100.0	273	100.0	42	100.0	226	100.0	104	100.0

	Total		Age Group					
			15–24		25–64		65+	
	f	%	f	%	f	%	f	%
Paris	151	30.3	58	41.4	90	28.2	3	7.7
New York	68	13.7	31	22.1	35	11.0	2	5.1
Dubai	41	8.2	10	7.1	31	9.7		
Beijing	16	3.2	5	3.6	11	3.4		
non	133	26.7	20	14.3	94	29.5	19	48.7
Don't know	42	8.4	8	5.7	28	8.8	6	15.4
irrelevant	47	9.4	8	5.7	30	9.4	9	23.1
Total	498	100.0	140	100.0	319	100.0	39	100.0

City respondents would most like to visit. Mecca was offered, but no one chose it.

Table 8.1. Abu Dhabi Television/Zogby Iran Poll, June 4, 2001 MOE +/– 4.5 Percentage Points (set 5 of 6)

	Iran Direction									
	Right Direction		Wrong Track		Not Sure		Don't Know		Irrelevant	
	f	%	f	%	f	%	f	%	f	%
Paris	55	31.1	48	27.6	24	44.4	11	17.7	12	40.0
New York	27	15.3	31	17.8	4	7.4	4	6.5	2	6.7
Dubai	16	9.0	14	8.0	1	1.9	8	12.9	2	6.7
Beijing	4	2.3	8	4.6			3	4.8	1	3.3
non	50	28.2	35	20.1	17	31.5	20	32.3	11	36.7
Don't know	13	7.3	17	9.8	5	9.3	6	9.7	1	3.3
irrelevant	12	6.8	21	12.1	3	5.6	10	16.1	1	3.3
Total	177	100.0	174	100.0	54	100.0	62	100.0	30	100.0

	Social Position					
	Upper		Middle		Lower	
	f	%	f	%	f	%
Paris	29	38.2	96	27.5	26	35.6
New York	15	19.7	45	12.9	8	11.0
Dubai	4	5.3	28	8.0	9	12.3
Beijing	2	2.6	11	3.2	3	4.1
non	9	11.8	101	28.9	23	31.5
Don't know	2	2.6	38	10.9	2	2.7
irrelevant	15	19.7	30	8.6	2	2.7
Total	76	100.0	349	100.0	73	100.0

City respondents would most like to visit, continued

	Gender				Status					
	Female		Male		Single		Married		Else	
	f	%	f	%	f	%	f	%	f	%
Paris	73	28.7	78	32.0	67	42.7	81	25.1	1	6.3
New York	28	11.0	40	16.4	34	21.7	33	10.2	1	6.3
Dubai	26	10.2	15	6.1	12	7.6	28	8.7	1	6.3
Beijing	4	1.6	12	4.9	8	5.1	8	2.5		
non	66	26.0	67	27.5	19	12.1	107	33.1	7	43.8
Don't know	25	9.8	17	7.0	6	3.8	35	10.8	1	6.3
irrelevant	32	12.6	15	6.1	11	7.0	31	9.6	5	31.3
Total	254	100.0	244	100.0	157	100.0	323	100.0	16	100.0

Table 8.1. Abu Dhabi Television/Zogby Iran Poll, June 4, 2001
MOE +/- 4.5 Percentage Points (set 6 of 6)

	Education						Ethnicity			
	Low		Middle		High		Fars		Other	
	f	%	f	%	f	%	f	%	f	%
Paris	1	3.2	122	30.3	27	45.0	99	29.3	51	32.5
New York			59	14.7	9	15.0	54	16.0	14	8.9
Dubai	2	6.5	35	8.7	4	6.7	27	8.0	13	8.3
Beijing			14	3.5	2	3.3	10	3.0	5	3.2
non	10	32.3	110	27.4	10	16.7	94	27.8	39	24.8
Don't know	10	32.3	29	7.2	3	5.0	28	8.3	14	8.9
irrelevant	8	25.8	33	8.2	5	8.3	26	7.7	21	13.4
Total	31	100.0	402	100.0	60	100.0	338	100.0	157	100.0

Mexico (2000)

We shook the world in Mexico in their July 2000 presidential election. There were three major candidates: Francisco Labastida of the left-wing Institutional Revolutionary Party (PRI), Vicente Fox of the conservative National Action Party (PAN), and revolutionary populist Andrés Manuel López Obrador, who as of this writing is now president many years later. It was very much a three-way race, but the PRI had ruled Mexico for seventy-one years, and no one expected that they could possibly lose, since our neighbor's elections had always been hopelessly corrupted in their favor.[5] All the polls showed small leads of four to five points by Labastida. We did our first poll for Reuters three weeks before the election and had Fox leading 46.3 percent to 41.6 percent. The Reuters-Zogby Poll was front-page news, with a picture of my international polling director, throughout the world. A poll we did ten days later showed Labastida in a statistical dead heat with Fox, but our initial poll had everyone—including us—on pins and needles.[6] Fox went on to win the election, and in addition to the numbers, we had some keen insights.

International organizations were closely monitoring this election to try to reduce the corruption that the ruling PRI had defined for seven decades. They always managed to bribe election officials and buy votes, especially among poverty-stricken rural voters. I felt confident in saying publicly that if the election was a fair one, Fox would win. This was because I probed more deeply into voter sentiment in both polls, especially among the huge numbers of rural poor, the longtime bedrock support base of the leftist PRI. I found in both polls that 72–74 percent of this group felt that things in Mexico were on the "wrong track." Less than 20 percent saw things on the "right track." And a mere 6 percent felt that they were "better off financially" than they were four years ago. This was the group that

Table 8.2.   Reuters/Zogby, Mexico, May 9, 2000—Likely Voters
Question: Overall would you say things in Mexico are headed in the right direction or are they on the wrong track?

	Total		pa) Zone				pb) Gender			
			Urban		Rural		Male		Female	
	f	%	f	%	f	%	f	%	f	%
Right directions	310	29.1	209	27.7	101	32.6	167	31.7	142	26.7
Wrong track	661	62.2	486	64.6	175	56.5	325	61.6	336	62.9
DK/NK	92	8.6	58	7.7	34	10.9	36	6.7	56	10.5
Total	1062	100.0	752	100.0	310	100.0	528	100.0	534	100.0

	pc) Color											
	NO CODED		White		Light Brown		Dark Brown		Black		other	
	f	%	f	%	f	%	f	%	f	%	f	%
Right directions	5	14.1	68	29.5	139	30.0	96	29.1	1	15.8	1	100.0
Wrong track	28	82.6	142	61.7	287	62.1	199	60.6	4	84.2		
DK/NK	1	3.3	20	8.8	36	7.8	34	10.3				
Total	33	100.0	231	100.0	462	100.0	329	100.0	5	100.0	1	100.0

	pd) What is your age?					
	18–29		30–49		50+	
	f	%	f	%	f	%
Right directions	112	27.3	129	30.3	69	30.4
Wrong track	270	65.8	257	60.4	134	59.2
DK/NK	28	6.9	39	9.3	24	10.4
Total	410	100.0	425	100.0	227	100.0

	pe) School grade									
	No Studies		Primary		Secondary		Preparatory		University	
	f	%	f	%	f	%	f	%	f	%
Right directions	25	25.3	116	29.3	82	32.5	52	26.7	35	28.7
Wrong track	62	62.0	237	59.9	156	61.9	126	64.9	81	66.5
DK/NK	13	12.7	43	10.8	14	5.6	16	8.4	6	4.8
Total	99	100.0	395	100.0	252	100.0	194	100.0	122	100.0

Labastida was counting on and that his party had always been able to subsidize at election time. For Mexico in 2000, corruption did not sway this election.[7]

PAN tried from the outset to make the election a referendum on seventy-plus years of PRI's heavy-handed rule and what that had done to the country's political institutions.[8] "We are proposing a transition to democracy to go from the regime of the last seventy years, with all its vices and corruption, to a true democracy," Fox had said in his public debate with Labastida, by all accounts winning.[9] The vote was deemed fair, and in the privacy of their polling booths, the people they termed "peasants" voted for change. In addition to the strong sentiments among these voters, other polling as well as ours showed that more than 62 percent of all voters felt that Mexico was on the wrong track. Also, 75.3 percent said their personal finances were either the same or worse than a year ago. Many civic organizations fielded more than eighty thousand trained electoral observers, and foreign observers—notably from both the United States and the European Union—were invited to witness the process. Numerous reports from observations and exit polls validated the official vote tabulation. Mexico had instituted electoral reforms in 1989, and this was the first time that there was an attempt to enforce them. For the first time in seven decades, Mexico had a transfer of power from one party to another.[10]

We came back in 2006 and nailed the very tight three-way race for the presidency.

Israel (1999)

I also polled in Israel in that time frame and called the Ariel Sharon victory in 2000 right on the nose. But my real story, as I briefly noted in an earlier chapter, was drawn from the 1999 election, in which, following the assassination of Prime Minister Yitzhak Rabin, the Labor Party's Ehud Barak and Likud's Benjamin Netanyahu tackled each other. We were commissioned by a proreform liberal organization in the United States to see whether there could be common ground, an intersection of messaging that could appeal to two diametrically opposed voting groups: Israeli Arabs, who normally have a lower voter turnout but lean toward the socialist Labor Party, and Russian Jews, who are very conservative and would be expected to support the rightist Likud Party. These two groups share little in common—the Russian Jews were relative newcomers; the Arabs had been there forever. I was particularly honored and pleased to have been selected to do this project because I am of Lebanese descent and I learned to appreciate both the culture and the politics of the region from my parents. Significantly for me, I had been known as an Arab-American activist and a cofounder of my brother's organization, the Arab American Institute, and it was gratifying that a pro-Israeli organization trusted me enough to produce honest results and analysis. It was neither the first nor the last time I would be called on to poll groups with differing viewpoints on this and other issues.

What we needed to find out was what messages could increase turnout among the Arabs and, *at the same time,* chip away at some Russian support for Netanyahu. We found this. They both shared a similar sentiment that they were underemployed and underappreciated. Among the forty questions we asked, we found that Russians, more recently arrived and with great expectations, had a deep sense that they were being exploited. Many had arrived highly educated and found themselves driving taxis, working on loading docks, and doing other forms of manual labor. The Arabs were always haunted by the fact that they were relegated to third-class citizenship. If Ehud Barak could address that common denominator, he would for once show a concern for two important groups that had been previously marginalized. The poll of Russian émigrés found that over 80 percent—overall and among all subgroups—felt that "understanding the needs of educated working people in Israel" was either the "most important" (half) or a "very important" (30 percent) issue to be addressed. In the separate survey of Israeli Arabs, over 90 percent said that understanding "professional Arabs with an education" was the most pressing issue (over 80 percent the "most important," another 10 percent "very important"). Building a bridge between two diametrically opposed (both ideologically and ethnically) groups would be no small task. The two groups resented each other—the Arabs for having been there for centuries, the Russian Jews for what they believed had become a false dream. "Underemployment" was the message. We passed that on to our client and then on to American strategist James Carville, who was working for Barak. On election day, Barak won decisively and was able to claim an enhanced turnout of Arab Israelis (from 12 percent of the vote to 15 percent of total votes cast) plus 20 percent of the Russian Jewish vote, the latter quite an accomplishment for a socialist candidate from the Labor Party.

Table 8.3. Zogby International, Israel Poll of Russians with an Education— Importance of Professional Jobs for Russians in the Election, April 27, 1999 (set 1 of 3)

| | Total | | 2. For which candidate did you vote in 1996? | | | | | | 3. How likely are you to vote in the May 17 election for Prime Minister? | | | |
| | | | Peres | | Netanyahu | | Other | | Very Lkly | | Smwt Lkly | |
	f	%	f	%	f	%	f	%	f	%	f	%
MostImp	271	54.2	78	52.0	168	54.4	20	66.7	209	55.4	58	53.2
VeryImp	147	29.4	45	30.0	93	30.1	7	23.3	108	28.6	32	29.4
SmwtImp	34	6.8	14	9.3	17	5.5	1	3.3	23	6.1	9	8.3
NotImp	22	4.4	5	3.3	16	5.2			17	4.5	4	3.7
NS	26	5.2	8	5.3	15	4.9	2	6.7	20	5.3	6	5.5
Total	500	100.0	150	100.0	309	100.0	30	100.0	377	100.0	109	100.0

Table 8.3. Zogby International, Israel Poll of Russians with an Education— Importance of Professional Jobs for Russians in the Election, April 27, 1999 (set 2 of 3)

	Occupation												
	White Collar		Blue Collar		Merchant		Student		Housewife		Unemployed		Other	
	f	%	f	%	f	%	f	%	f	%	f	%	f	%
MostImp	102	52.3	76	52.8	12	50.0	9	52.9	11	44.0	47	69.1	9	64.3
VeryImp	57	29.2	46	31.9	8	33.3	5	29.4	7	28.0	15	22.1	4	28.6
SmwtImp	17	8.7	7	4.9	2	8.3	1	5.9	1	4.0	4	5.9	1	7.1
NotImp	7	3.6	10	6.9	2	8.3	1	5.9	2	8.0				
NS	12	6.2	5	3.5			1	5.9	4	16.0	2	2.9		
Total	195	100.0	144	100.0	24	100.0	17	100.0	25	100.0	68	100.0	14	100.0

	4. For whom would you vote from the following . . .?											
	Netanyahu		Barak		Mordechai		Begin		Bishara		NS	
	f	%	f	%	f	%	f	%	f	%	f	%
MostImp	103	50.5	52	50.0	8	53.3	3	30.0	1	100.0	103	62.4
VeryImp	63	30.9	32	30.8	5	33.3	5	50.0			42	25.5
SmwtImp	18	8.8	6	5.8	2	13.3	2	20.0			6	3.6
NotImp	12	5.9	7	6.7							3	1.8
NS	8	3.9	7	6.7							11	6.7
Total	204	100.0	104	100.0	15	100.0	10	100.0	1	100.0	165	100.0

	7. Party								Gender			
	Likud		Labor Party		Another Party		NS		Male		Female	
	f	%	f	%	f	%	f	%	f	%	f	%
MostImp	83	56.1	34	56.7	87	52.7	66	52.4	136	53.3	134	55.6
VeryImp	41	27.7	18	30.0	48	29.1	40	31.7	73	28.6	71	29.5
SmwtImp	12	8.1	4	6.7	12	7.3	6	4.8	18	7.1	16	6.6
NotImp	9	6.1	1	1.7	9	5.5	3	2.4	17	6.7	5	2.1
NS	3	2.0	3	5.0	9	5.5	11	8.7	11	4.3	15	6.2
Total	148	100.0	60	100.0	165	100.0	126	100.0	255	100.0	241	100.0

	Total		19. Personal/Household Finances											
			Much Better		Smwt Better		Same		Smwt Worse		Much Worse		NS	
	f	%	f	%	f	%	f	%	f	%	f	%	f	%
MostImp	271	54.2	13	59.1	70	51.9	126	55.5	45	60.0	14	53.8	3	21.4
VeryImp	147	29.4	5	22.7	37	27.4	71	31.3	19	25.3	10	38.5	5	35.7
SmwtImp	34	6.8	1	4.5	15	11.1	12	5.3	4	5.3			1	7.1

Table 8.3. Zogby International, Israel Poll of Russians with an Education— Importance of Professional Jobs for Russians in the Election, April 27, 1999 (set 3 of 3)

| | Total | | 19. Personal/Household Finances | | | | | | | | | | |
| | | | Much Better | | Smwt Better | | Same | | Smwt Worse | | Much Worse | | NS | |
	f	%	f	%	f	%	f	%	f	%	f	%	f	%
NotImp	22	4.4	2	9.1	5	3.7	9	4.0	4	5.3	1	3.8	1	7.1
NS	26	5.2	1	4.5	8	5.9	9	4.0	3	4.0	1	3.8	4	28.6
Total	500	100.0	22	100.0	135	100.0	227	100.0	75	100.0	26	100.0	14	100.0

| | 20. Israel Direction | | | | | | Religion | | | | | |
| | Right Dir | | WrongD ir | | NS | | Orthodox | | Conservative | | Non Observant | |
	f	%	f	%	f	%	f	%	f	%	f	%
MostImp	85	50.9	96	59.6	90	52.3			25	44.6	220	56.8
VeryImp	55	32.9	46	28.6	46	26.7	1	50.0	21	37.5	108	27.9
SmwtImp	13	7.8	5	3.1	16	9.3	1	50.0	4	7.1	27	7.0
NotImp	9	5.4	6	3.7	7	4.1			3	5.4	17	4.4
NS	5	3.0	8	5.0	13	7.6			3	5.4	15	3.9
Total	167	100.0	161	100.0	172	100.0	2	100.0	56	100.0	387	100.0

| | Age | | | | | | | |
| | 18–29 | | 30–49 | | 50–64 | | 65+ | |
	f	%	f	%	f	%	f	%
MostImp	36	45.0	90	48.6	88	61.1	57	62.6
VeryImp	23	28.8	64	34.6	38	26.4	22	24.2
SmwtImp	9	11.3	12	6.5	9	6.3	4	4.4
NotImp	5	6.3	9	4.9	5	3.5	3	3.3
NS	7	8.8	10	5.4	4	2.8	5	5.5
Total	80	100.0	185	100.0	144	100.0	91	100.0

| | Income | | | | | | | | | | | |
| | MMore Average | | More Average | | Same | | Less Average | | MLess Average | | NS | |
	f	%	f	%	f	%	f	%	f	%	f	%
MostImp	4	26.7	25	50.0	92	58.6	96	61.5	39	48.8	12	31.6
VeryImp	7	46.7	18	36.0	38	24.2	43	27.6	26	32.5	15	39.5
SmwtImp	1	6.7	4	8.0	16	10.2	7	4.5	1	1.3	5	13.2
NotImp	2	13.3	2	4.0	6	3.8	6	3.8	6	7.5		
NS	1	6.7	1	2.0	5	3.2	4	2.6	8	10.0	6	15.8
Total	15	100.0	50	100.0	157	100.0	156	100.0	80	100.0	38	100.0

Table 8.4. Zogby International, Israel Poll of Arabs with an Education—Importance of Professional Jobs for Arabs in the Election, April 27, 1999 (set 1 of 3)

	7. Party									
	Total		Likud		Labor Party		Another Party		NS	
	f	%	f	%	f	%	f	%	f	%
MostImp	413	82.1	13	68.4	193	84.3	162	87.1	45	65.2
VeryImp	64	12.7	4	21.1	32	14.0	22	11.8	6	8.7
SmwtImp	5	1.0	1	5.3	2	.9	2	1.1		
NotImp	2	.4	1	5.3					1	1.4
NS	19	3.8			2	.9			17	24.6
Total	503	100.0	19	100.0	229	100.0	186	100.0	69	100.0

	Age							
	18–29		30–49		50–64		65+	
	f	%	f	%	f	%	f	%
MostImp	179	84.4	174	79.8	49	84.5	11	73.3
VeryImp	22	10.4	32	14.7	7	12.1	3	20.0
SmwtImp	2	.9	2	.9			1	6.7
NotImp			2	.9				
NS	9	4.2	8	3.7	2	3.4		
Total	212	100.0	218	100.0	58	100.0	15	100.0

	Income									
	MMore Average		More Average		Same		Less Average		MLess Average	
	f	%	f	%	f	%	f	%	f	%
MostImp	31	81.6	82	84.5	91	77.1	141	87.6	47	79.7
VeryImp	3	7.9	12	12.4	19	6.1	14	8.7	9	15.3
SmwtImp	1	2.6			2	1.7	1	.6	1	1.7
NotImp			1	1.0	1	.8				
NS	3	7.9	2	2.1	5	4.2	5	3.1	2	3.4
Total	38	100.0	97	100.0	118	100.0	161	100.0	59	100.0

	Gender						Religion							
	Total		Male		Female		Muslim		Christian		Druze		Other	
	f	%	f	%	f	%	f	%	f	%	f	%	f	%
MostImp	404	82.4	203	80.6	201	84.5	242	85.8	95	84.8	35	60.3	30	83.3
VeryImp	60	12.2	36	14.3	24	10.1	35	12.4	11	9.8	12	20.7	4	11.1
SmwtImp	5	1.0	3	1.2	2	.8	1	.4	1	.9	3	5.2		
NotImp	2	.4			2	.8			1	.9				
NS	19	3.9	10	4.0	9	3.8	4	1.4	4	3.6	8	13.8	2	5.6
Total	490	100.0	252	100.0	238	100.0	282	100.0	112	100.0	58	100.0	36	100.0

Table 8.4. Zogby International, Israel Poll of Arabs with an Education— Importance of Professional Jobs for Arabs in the Election, April 27, 1999 (set 2 of 3)

| | Occupation | | | | | | | | | | | | |
| | White Collar | | Blue Collar | | Merchant | | Student | | Housewife | | Unemployed | | Other | |
	f	%	f	%	f	%	f	%	f	%	f	%	f	%
MostImp	78	82.1	89	75.4	23	85.2	31	88.6	79	84.9	39	84.8	49	84.5
VeryImp	11	11.6	22	18.6	4	14.8	2	5.7	12	12.9	3	6.5	5	8.6
SmwtImp	1	1.1	1	.8							1	2.2	2	3.4
NotImp	2	2.1												
NS	3	3.2	6	5.1			2	5.7	2	2.2	3	6.5	2	3.4
Total	95	100.0	118	100.0	27	100.0	35	100.0	93	100.0	46	100.0	58	100.0

| | 7. Party | | | | | | | | | |
| | Total | | Likud | | Labor Party | | Another Party | | NS | |
	f	%	f	%	f	%	f	%	f	%
Netanyahu	16	3.2	13	68.4	1	.4	2	1.1		
Barak	218	43.3	2	10.5	142	62.0	57	30.6	17	24.6
Mordechai	46	91	2	10.5	18	7.9	21	11.3	5	7.2
Begin										
Bishara	132	26.2			39	17.0	80	43.0	13	18.8
NS	91	18.1	2	10.5	29	12.7	26	14.0	34	49.3
Total	503	100.0	19	100.0	229	100.0	186	100.0	69	100.0

| | Age | | | | | | | |
| | 18–29 | | 30–49 | | 50–64 | | 65+ | |
	f	%	f	%	f	%	f	%
Netanyahu	5	2.4	8	3.7	3	5.2		
Barak	98	46.2	90	41.3	22	37.9	8	53.3
Mordechai	15	7.1	21	9.6	8	13.8	2	13.3
Begin								
Bishara	55	25.9	59	27.1	15	25.9	3	20.0
NS	39	18.4	40	18.3	10	17.2	2	13.3
Total	212	100.0	218	100.0	58	100.0	15	100.0

| | Income | | | | | | | | | |
| | MMore Average | | More Average | | Same | | Less Average | | MLess Average | |
	f	%	f	%	f	%	f	%	f	%
Netanyahu	1	2.6	3	3.1	4	3.4	5	3.1	2	3.4
Barak	16	42.1	51	52.6	57	48.3	64	39.8	19	32.2
Mordechai	2	5.3	10	10.3	11	9.3	11	6.8	8	13.6

Table 8.4. Zogby International, Israel Poll of Arabs with an Education—Importance of Professional Jobs for Arabs in the Election, April 27, 1999 (set 3 of 3)

	Income									
	MMore Average		More Average		Same		Less Average		MLess Average	
	f	%	f	%	f	%	f	%	f	%
Begin										
Bishara	9	23.7	21	21.6	22	18.6	55	34.2	17	28.8
NS	10	26.3	12	12.4	24	20.3	26	16.1	13	22.0
Total	38	100.0	97	100.0	118	100.0	161	100.0	59	100.0

	Gender					
	Total		Male		Female	
	f	%	f	%	f	%
Netanyahu	16	3.3	7	2.8	9	3.8
Barak	211	43.1	112	44.4	99	41.6
Mordechai	45	9.2	23	9.1	22	9.2
Begin						
Bishara	130	26.5	67	26.6	63	26.5
NS	88	18.0	43	17.1	45	18.9
Total	490	100.0	52	100.0	238	100.0

	Religion							
	Muslim		Christian		Druze		Other	
	f	%	f	%	f	%	f	%
Netanyahu	9	3.2			6	10.3		
Barak	128	45.4	47	42.0	20	34.5	18	50.0
Mordechai	24	8.5	12	10.7	6	10.3	1	2.8
Begin								
Bishara	90	31.9	27	24.1	3	5.2	10	27.8
NS	31	11.0	26	23.2	23	39.7	7	19.4
Total	282	100.0	112	100.0	58	100.0	36	100.0

	Occupation													
	White Collar		Blue Collar		Merchant		Student		Housewife		Unemployed		other	
	f	%	f	%	f	%	f	%	f	%	f	%	f	%
Netanyahu	3	3.2	3	2.5	2	7.4	3	8.6	3	3.2	1	2.2	1	1.7
Barak	42	44.2	58	49.2	16	59.3	12	34.3	36	38.7	22	47.8	17	29.3
Mordechai	6	6.3	13	11.0	2	7.4	2	5.7	11	11.8	5	10.9	4	6.9
Begin														
Bishara	27	28.4	24	20.3	4	14.8	9	25.7	30	32.3	9	19.6	23	39.7
NS	17	17.9	20	16.9	3	11.1	9	25.7	13	14.0	9	19.6	13	22.4
Total	95	100.0	118	100.0	27	100.0	35	100.0	93	100.0	46	100.0	58	100.0

Albania (2009)

The Albanian election of June 2009 was really a great challenge for us. This would be only their second democratic election since the fall of Communism, and the idea of conducting opinion polls was still very alien. The small country, which borders Greece, Montenegro, Kosovo, and both the Adriatic and the Ionian Seas, was seeking membership in the European Union. It needed to show that it could hold a clean and free election and then make some progress on democratic reforms like transparency and criminal justice. The election for 140 seats would be a major step forward. We had been asked by Top Channel, the leading news network based in the capital city of Tirana, to submit a proposal to do seven monthly preelection polls plus an election day exit poll.

I was in Miami in February when we were notified that we had won the contract. Since most of the details had been worked out by the terrific folks in our Washington office, I was not yet deeply familiar with all facets of the proposed project when the call came in. It happened the very same day that we were awarded the contract, and they asked me whether I could be interviewed in a couple of hours by Top Channel at a television studio in Coral Gables. I put on a blue blazer over a polo shirt and shorts and requested a car service to take me to a studio that Top Channel found. They wanted me live on their 10:00 p.m. news broadcast to discuss the polling. It all happened so fast, and I was, of course, stuck in traffic on the overcrowded Route 1 leading from downtown Miami en route to the studio in Coral Gables. I arrived just in time to sit, get a mic and earpiece, and be introduced by a translator.

First question: "Mr. Zogby, it is said that you bring a bias to your polling and that you will clearly favor your party in this election."

My reply was quick. "Sir, I am not even sure of who is running yet. I cannot possibly be biased."

I was not trying to be disrespectful, just honest. A total of seventy-one parliamentary seats were needed by a party or coalition to govern with a majority. Our results—and the final election count—showed seventy seats for the Democratic alliance, which had won the previous election, and sixty-nine seats for the Socialist alliance, with one disputed. That final seat was not resolved until months later.

Essentially, we hired a university team in Tirana to conduct the actual fieldwork and sent one of our statisticians, who was from Eastern Europe, along with a project manager from our office in Washington. We mapped out the country into quadrants, with random sampling points in each quadrant that ensured that cities and villages were equitably represented. We also trained the field supervisors to be extra vigilant to ensure that there were no side deals. A *New York Times* series back in 1997 had reported that in parts of Tirana, and largely outside of the capital, folks were still using horses and buggies for transportation, and the article expressed concern that many were heavily reliant on Ponzi schemes for income. Data was collected on laptops and transported to Utica to be cleaned and validated. Any discrepancies or questions were reported to our team on the ground. But the bottom line was that while a majority felt let down by the governing Socialists, who were corrupt, they felt that the Democratic coalition was equally corrupt and also retrograde.

Fortunately, my team and I had more time to study what was going on, get our feet on the ground, and conduct a series of monthly polls. By mid-June, we produced both a remarkably accurate final preelection poll and a perfect exit poll. We have had great success in calling elections outside (and inside) the United States and had success again in Albania. Our preelection poll found the ruling Democratic Party holding a two-point lead over its main opposition, the Socialist Party. As a coalition, however, the Democrats were in a statistical dead heat with the Socialists. We were comfortable projecting Democrats would win 69 out of the total 140 seats, with twelve other seats too close to call.[11] The Albanian election was close, with the vote a one-point win for the Democratic coalition, which filled seventy of the seats.

In earlier monthly polls, Albanian voters were about evenly split on whether the country was headed in the right direction. By our mid-June poll, 51 percent said things were going in the right direction, while 38 percent said they were not. Now, during the course of our polling for this election, we found a growing sense that the country was headed in the right direction, and support for the ruling party was solid among those who told us they felt that way. In addition, people under thirty were not enamored with the Socialist Party, even though pundits had suggested the much younger Socialist candidate would do well with this age group.[12]

So, despite a recent history of distrust and notwithstanding its past dictatorship, voters in Albania were willing to talk honestly about their ballots face-to-face with an independent polling company. Albanians have come a long way. Expressing their opinions appeared to be liberating and a sign that democracy, as messy as it may be, could be taking hold. As I told *Research Live* magazine, "The very fact that (our) firm was able to conduct an accurate exit poll in the vote on 28 June said a lot about the state of democracy and readiness for reform in Albania, where past elections have been criticized by observers."[13]

The country was, as the results showed, evenly split, and the results on issues and future reflected this split. The significance of the procedure was that Albania had a democratic election, fought a battle over the legitimacy of the disputed seat and the majority, but life went on. And we were able to provide a useful record of public sentiment that documented why the results made sense.

Tunisia (2011)

Tunisia held its first democratic election since its independence in 1956. It launched the Arab Spring in late 2010, which spread throughout the Arab world. Following this event, the election in October 2011 was for a representative Constituent Assembly whose main task was to write a constitution for the country. Under the brutal strongman Zine El Abidine Ben Ali, Islamists had been repressed, and the fear both inside Tunisia and throughout the world was that the country would revert to an ultraconservative regime that punished women and was hostile to trade with the West. As in most autocracies, opposition was banned, and there were few leaders waiting in the wings to grab the mantle of twenty-first-century leadership. In addition, the economy was in a severe slowdown, and tourism, which was a leading industry in this very beautiful Mediterranean haven, had ground to a halt.[14]

The leading party in the election was Ennahda, a center-right and moderately Islamist organization led by a longtime exiled ultraconservative named Rached Ghannouchi. Ghannouchi was promising a liberal (i.e., free enterprise and free trade) economy and a greater role for Islam in public life. Tunisia had been somewhat modernized under its previous leadership. Its longtime leader since its independence, Habib Bourguiba, had modeled his rule after Turkey's post–World War I secular and modernist strongman Mustafa Kemal Atatürk, but Ghannouchi pronouncements over the years from Paris were troubling to secularists. There were several other opposition parties, but Ennahda was comfortably leading in polls.[15]

I was brought in as a pollster/consultant for the Progressive Democratic Party, a well-funded, secular, socially liberal party led by a professor named Maya Jribi. Jribi was a strong, capable party leader who possessed absolutely no charisma. She was a longtime opponent of the previous regime and an ardent feminist, but my observation of her in party leadership meetings was that she could have led what is commonly referred to as a technocratic government but could never be elected to office. Like Ghannouchi, who had placed someone else in the position of candidate to lead the party in the Assembly, Jribi and her team put up Ahmed Najib Chebbi, a well-known attorney, opponent of the Ben Ali regime, and party founder, as their candidate. Chebbi was in his sixties, tall and blue-eyed, and oozed charisma. But he had no real political experience as a candidate and, like his party, was revered by the business community but not popular with voters. As an example of this challenge, I once observed him campaigning in a rural village, and he suggested to those of us with him that he felt he needed a shower after the visit.

We did daily tracking for a month and two dozen focus groups. The polling always showed a strong plurality supporting Ennahda, while Chebbi topped off at 10 percent. There were other parties that were drawing single-digit support. But this was a pivotal election. Tunisia could very well have been a bellwether for the ultimate future of the Arab Spring. Our focus groups were very revealing. They were composed mainly of men and women under thirty-five years of age—the overwhelming majority of their nation (and all other nations in their region). Women who were fully covered were seated with those in miniskirts who worked in business or studied in universities.

The main issue for both men and women was the economy and their personal future. Many were very proud that they had participated in the overthrow of the Ben Ali government. Some had actually participated in the demonstrations in Tunis's relatively small Bourguiba Square, but most held up their smartphones to show that they had been tweeting updates to each other and to the world. One woman said, "Do the American kids think we are cool?"

But underlying both their economic concerns and their initial optimism was the fear of descending into chaos. What would happen next? Could Tunisia rejoin the global economy? Would they secure jobs and promotions? Would ultraconservative Salafists continue their campaign of attacking women in broad daylight with impunity? They seemed to be equally worried about Ghannouchi enabling these Islamist monsters versus the disorganization of a party or coalition that had no experience governing.

In the final analysis, Ghannouchi did win. The sense of a bright Arab Spring had waned. The economy was sour. Fear reigned supreme. Ghannouchi and Ennahda won big with 37 percent of the vote. The nearest rival came in at 9 percent. Ennahda was organized; it had a network and a base. It seemed to promise some order and security. The young rebels, as well as their counterparts who just wanted a semblance of security, perhaps some cooling off until the next phase for Tunisia, seemed to be satisfied for the moment.

As things turned out, the Arab Spring died in Egypt, Libya, and especially Syria. In all instances, sectarianism and brutality were victorious. Libya today is a failed state. Syria is more repressive and even murderous. Egypt is again dominated by a totalitarian regime, as it had been under Anwar Sadat and Hosni Mubarak. The great Tunisian experiment is evolving with ebbs and flows. But it at least has not descended into the hell of the other countries. In the final analysis, the legacy of dictators and no tradition of democracy is the destruction of opposition—and, thus, any real alternative but chaos.[16]

The polling in Tunisia was accurate enough, but the focus groups presented a much more holistic view. By the way, I have always prided myself on the fact that I have lived a lifetime in Utica, something I feel has grounded me in political reality. I got to visit Utica, Tunisia—close to where Chebbi had visited. Again, that was all I really needed to get the picture.[17]

Lessons from Chapter 8

I am amazed at how many times communities or nations that are diverse in population, split over needs and ideas, and partisan by birth, choice, or circumstances end up with a clear message to leaders and pollsters. Often the message blends into one voice, despite the variety of sources. In each of the above instances, voters in these nations spoke with independence and defied the conventional wisdom that was generated by elites who were too often myopic in their insular cocoons. In Iran, despite news blackouts and heavy-handed Revolutionary Guards, voters never abandoned their quest for modernization and freedom. In Mexico, voters of all classes were ready to put the brakes on corruption and tyranny. In Albania, voters were honestly split over the future but opted for the devil they knew. And in Tunisia, they were ultimately tired of the chaos and unpredictability of the revolution and needed time to cool off.

Whenever possible, we have to do the best we can to adhere to the conventional rules. At the same time, when we go overseas, we also have to remember that, like Dorothy, "we're not in Kansas anymore." The poll in Iran involved some creative rule breaking. The tracking polls we did in Tunisia were done via mobile phones. Honestly, if a revolution can happen by mobile technology, can't a poll be done the same way? In both cases, the polls were correct. In another manuscript I tell the story about how we were the first to poll Iraqis during the war. Our colleagues on the ground were shot at in A Ramadi, near Saddam Hussein's hometown west of Baghdad, engaged in a high-speed car chase on the way to Basra in the south, and detained in the home of a local sheikh until they could prove they were not with the Central Intelligence Agency. We no sooner released our findings than AAPOR representatives attacked the poll as not a random probability sample but a "convenience sample." Does that sound very "convenient" to you? My response? "Go to Iraq and do a better poll." Ironically, it was two senior employees at Gallup, the dean of polling and generic brand name for polling conventions, who wrote the bestselling management book *First, Break All the Rules*.[18] There were times I had to do just that. Or some of them, anyway.

And then there was the time I joined with my alma mater, Le Moyne College, and was asked to poll United States servicemen and women deployed in Iraq. Boy, that was such a great poll! We found four bases, with men and women from all branches of service, where the cooks were Lebanese. We arranged through our field team to pay the cooks to distribute and collect the surveys confidentially. We found that most of the deployed could not state with accuracy what their mission was in Iraq and wanted the United States out of that country within a year. Critics said it was not a random probability sample. In the purest sense, it wasn't. But the results told an important story of at least those four bases.

I have always enjoyed the opportunity to read the deeper meaning of the polls—to go beyond the simple winners and losers and attempt to find the deeper message that emerges when we speak to folks by the hundreds and thousands. When presented with the data, don't be afraid to riff, to combine your own experiences, interactions, and studies and weave the real story you find.

In each of the above instances, I found the use of metaphors and having feet on the ground to be necessary. In Iran, I required something to illuminate me on the minds and hearts of Iranians. The vote was indeed lopsided, but just who were these people who were going to vote? Were they angry? Did they really want reform? Or were they only thinking of the moment? Of course, we were limited by what we could ask, so the simple metaphor of the favorite city was designed to tell us a lot by only asking a little. And we learned once again that despite burkas, thought police, and Revolutionary Guards, there was a pro-modernization sentiment behind their choice. The shah's brutal regime was not going to deliver that by force and by being in the pocket of the United States and the West. But these folks wanted a new era.

In Mexico, we had to tread carefully. Believe it or not, our neighbor to the south was not accustomed to a peaceful transition to power or to independent jurisprudence. The election in 2000 was pivotal, and our poll was the first real indication that it could happen. We also had to be very careful, because poor people were not accustomed to expressing their own views or to voting how they really felt. When they expressed that they were really doing worse financially and that the country was on the wrong track, they were telling us that if their vote was secret, they were prepared to abandon their support for a hopelessly corrupt political party that had dominated Mexico for seven decades.

In Albania, the country was evenly split and neither candidate was beloved. And we were walking into a situation in which our high-profile client, as well as the political parties, watched our polling closely. As in Mexico, there was no history of free elections. Sending two of my best employees was itself a commitment by my company to show my client how serious we were about this project and that we were fearless about the results.

And in Tunisia, we were polling in the middle of a revolution. Not everyone gets to do that. This time, I was there not only to flesh out the meaning of the polls but also to bear witness to the difficulty of making a choice that none had ever made before. I could answer why, despite antipathy toward an Islamic party, these young people would ultimately choose it. I could also feel the excitement of how these young folks wanted the world and history to see them. Imagine, they wanted to know whether the American kids thought they were cool.

The examples I included in this chapter each represent more than a simple election result. In the cases of Mexico, Iran, Tunisia, and Albania, we were able to discover a readiness for democratic change simply through the way people were eager to respond to our carefully posed questions. In Israel, we discovered opportunities for bridge building between two radically different ethnic groups.

CHAPTER 9

Polling Is Very Much Alive

The most dangerous words in any profession these days are "We are going to conduct business the way we always have." Polling and market research are challenged by new technologies and societal behaviors that did not exist when I started in 1984. But polling is not dead. It is as vibrant, useful, and vital as ever. In fact, it is necessary, and that is why opinion research continues to grow. Sure, some of us do elections, but we actually do much more than just that. Our data offers context, texture, perspective, and a peek into the future. We provide a check and balance against wild and biased opinions by demagogues. We often serve up real surprises. And true opinion research is not collecting credit card receipts, observing facial gestures during a movie, or closely watching a shopper at the frozen food aisle. All of that is useful, but it doesn't capture the holistic view of people that we try to collect.

On the flip side, we are not God—or His/Her designated vicars. We are limited, and both we pollsters and the public need to recognize this fact. I can never forget the most powerful chapter in twentieth-century polymath Jacob Bronowski's book (and PBS series) *The Ascent of Man*, "Knowledge vs. Certainty."[1] Good science is wonderful, liberating, and progressive. But we can never have the hubris to pretend that we possess the truth. Even more important, we can never present our "truth" as a force to control, direct, or punish people. Bronowski offered these thoughts standing in a mud puddle at Auschwitz, where those who would control and destroy other peoples enacted their "Final Solution."

In looking at polls and opinion research, let's remember what they do, not what they cannot do (at least all the time). Let's be careful about expectations. Even when we share the results before an election—and I have done that and enjoyed it many times—we simply are not predicting. We are only capturing the moment—indeed, near the closing moments—in a campaign. After all, around 10–14 percent say they make up their minds at the last minute, and our results are one or two days before. Sure, there are times when we nail an election to the percentile. I have been fortunate to have experienced this result many times in my career. But I have always known that such is not the essence of what I am or what I do.

"Getting it right" is really about capturing the trend, projecting what may be next, finding the context, and answering the "why" questions. It cannot be about chasing the final results of an election to the percentile. We pollsters as a profession are guilty of pretending to be God and feeding a false narrative about that idea. What we really should be doing is a better job of explaining how we see the world we live in (and our fellow human beings) to others.

Today, there is an endless capacity to collect data, and there are both academic and practical applications for "data analytics." In addition, polls can be conducted via mobile technologies in shorter time frames than ever before. But analytics are only as good as the analyst. And the chief requirement on that résumé must include "well-read, multiexperienced, empathic human being." Data dumping and zippy charts don't help clients. Conclusions, directions, next steps, projections, and relationships do.

I am reminded of Zeno's paradox. Greek philosopher Plato relates the story of Zeno, a pre-Socrates philosopher who argued that, based on his "data," it is impossible for a runner to finish a race. First, he must traverse half the distance to the finish, which takes a finite time; then he must traverse half of the remaining distance, which takes a shorter time; and so on. Reaching the finish line would require an infinite number of finite times, and so the race can never be won.[2]

The point is, of course, if you get too far into the hard data alone, you never get to finish the race.

For years, after speaking to thousands of students all over the world, I have been asked how best to prepare to become a professional pollster. My reply has always been simple: Regardless of your major, load up on the humanities—history, literature, the classics—because here is where you not only plumb the depths of who people really are internally, as well as in context, but also learn the importance of language and expression. If we become populated by computerized data analysts and technical reporting, then we will truly lose our humanity.

Second, read novels—the old ones, the new ones, the ones on shelves at CVS, the ones you pay a dime for at garage sales. These are real characters, with real experiences, with inner selves bared to us, acting out situations, who survive, strategize, fall victim to their own demons, or thrive amid adversity. There is no better way to accumulate human stories than by letting the novelist do a lot of the heavy lifting for you.

Finally, volunteer for a political campaign. It makes no difference whether you like a candidate or hate politics; you get to observe situations in which people act in the context of something they believe in. And when I say "volunteer," don't ask to be chief strategist or communications director. Rather, be the so-called "Jimmy Higgins," the legendary and eponymous fictional volunteer in an Upton Sinclair novel.[3] He moved in American left-wing circles and thrived on knocking on doors, handing out flyers in the rain, and doing menial tasks. Get your hands dirty while you learn.

Above all, to the student, the academic researcher, the chief marketing officer, the CEO, whoever you are: *Be curious. Think like an end user. Don't be afraid to ask lots of questions. I've made a living out of doing that for almost forty years.*

I am reminded of a great novel that perhaps no one else ever read. Eugene Burdick (famous for his previous book with William Lederer in the 1950s, *The Ugly American*) published a novel in 1964 called *The 480*.[4] Written before the political tumult following the 1963 assassination of President John F. Kennedy, the novel features a fictitious charismatic figure, John Thatch, an engineer infected with the "political virus" who is seeking the Republican Party nomination for president in the 1964 election. Alas, because of the trauma of the assassination itself, the book did poorly. In the plot, a small cabal of political professionals are pushing Thatch's nomination. The slick consultants use mainframe computers to run massive simulations, which predict the public reaction to certain (proposed) political moves before they are implemented. These simulations make it easy to manipulate each of the "480"—that is, the separate groups (by party affiliation, socioeconomic status, location, origin, etc.) that the computer uses to classify the American electorate. The corporation and the computers they use in the novel were based on a new program that actually existed but was untried in real life at the time. The upshot in the book is that the data misses some key elements of the character of both the fictional candidate and parts of the electorate, so Thatch has to drop out of the race. The book was fiction, but it prefigured the work of analytical consultants today in both politics and business. And the lessons should be very clear: *No matter how complicated and exciting it may seem, do not generate data that is so limited in scope and so granular that it doesn't really mean anything, even if it sounds good. You lose the forest for the trees. And you may never reach the wall, as Zeno predicted.*

In terms of my profession, one short survey, a focus group, and a decent dose of experience with real people could have determined that, as the old joke goes about the world's best scientists designing the perfect dog food, the "dogs just didn't like it" (and saved a lot of time and money). Speaking of saving money, I picked up *The 480* at a garage sale in the village of Indian Lake, New York. So I practice what I preached to you.

For me, however, there is one key takeaway for those of you who have read any or all of this book. I have worked with statistics, and I do like numbers. But in the work that I do, I try to approach each respondent as a person with a heart and a story—not as a data point. This method grounds me. And I approach collective results not only as simple percentages but also as representations of the will of a community, as opportunities to solve problems, and as umbrellas covering lots of stories. Whether you are a student preparing for a life as an analyst, a business executive or manager who is in charge of motivating people, a human resources professional, a college or university professor, or a more general office employee, always remember that you are not simply working with data. *Everyone you deal with is a complex person with his or her own driving force. Try to never forget that.*

Notes

Chapter 1

1. Richard L. Hasen, *The Voting Wars: From Florida 2000 to the Next Election Melt-down* (New Haven, CT: Yale University Press, 2012), 20.

2. Diana C. Mutz, "Effects of Horse-Race Coverage on Campaign Coffers: Strategic Contributing in Presidential Primaries," *Journal of Politics* 57, no. 4 (November 1995): 1015–42. See also Thomas E. Patterson, "Of Polls, Mountains: US Journalists and Their Use of Election Surveys," *Public Opinion Quarterly* 69, no. 5 (2005): 716–24.

3. "Bush Up by 3 in MSNBC/Reuters/Zogby Tracking Poll," *White House Bulletin*, November 2, 2000.

4. "Bush Up by 5 in MSNBC/Reuters/Zogby Tracking Poll," *White House Bulletin*, November 1, 2000.

5. W. Joseph Campbell, *Lost in a Gallup: Polling Failure in U.S. Presidential Elections* (Berkeley: University of California Press, 2020), 140.

6. Editors, "Gore Ahead by 2 in MSNBC/Reuters/Zogby Tracking Poll," *The Bulletin's Frontrunner*, November 7, 2000.

7. John Kenneth White, with a foreword by John Zogby, *The Values Divide: American Politics and Culture in Transition* (New York: Chatham House, 2003), 64. See also Adam Clymer, "Poll Shows a Married Single Gap in Last Election," *New York Times*, January 6, 1983, section A, 12; Janet M. Box-Steffensmeier, Suzanna De Boef, and Tse-Min Lin, "The Dynamics of the Partisan Gender Gap," *American Political Science Review* 98, no. 3 (2004): 515–28.

8. John Zogby, *The Way We'll Be: The Zogby Report on the Transformation of the American Dream* (New York: Random House, 2008), 185. See also Kevin Munger, "The Emergence of Cohort Consciousness," chap. 7 in *Generation Gap: Why the Baby Boomers Still Dominate American Politics and Culture* (New York: Columbia University Press, 2022).

9. Zogby, *The Way We'll Be*. See also Robert Hudson, *The New Politics of Old Age Policy* (Baltimore, MD: Johns Hopkins University Press, 2014), 10.

10. Editors, "Gore Ahead by 2."

11. Editors, "Zogby Most Accurate Predictor of Presidential Results," *The Bulletin's Frontrunner*, November 9, 2000.

12. Jonathan N. Wand, Kenneth W. Shotts, Jasjeet S. Sekhon, Walter R. Mebane, Michael C. Herron, and Henry E. Brady, "The Butterfly Did It: The Aberrant Vote for Buchanan in Palm Beach County, Florida," *American Political Science Review* 95, no. 4 (2001): 793–810. See also Henry E. Bracy, Michael C. Herron, Walter R. Mebane Jr., and Jasjeet Singh Sekhon, "Law and Data: The Butterfly Ballot Episode," *PS: Political Science & Politics* 34, no. 1 (2001): 64.

13. Lynn Hudson Parsons, *The Birth of Modern Politics: Andrew Jackson, John Quincy Adams, and the Election of 1828* (New York: Oxford University Press, 2009), 78–79.

14. James M. McPherson, *Abraham Lincoln* (New York: Oxford University Press, 2009), 22.

15. Byron E. Shafer and Richard Johnston, *The End of Southern Exceptionalism: Class, Race, and Partisan Change in the Postwar South* (Cambridge, MA: Harvard University Press, 2009), 13, 14, 132.

16. "Poll Update—Reuters/Zogby: 60% Say If Gore Wins, He Stole the Election," *The Hotline (National Journal)*, November 27, 2000.

17. This trend has only increased over time. See Lilliana Mason, *Uncivil Agreement: How Politics Became Our Identity* (Chicago: University of Chicago Press, 2018).

18. Alan Abramowitz, *The Great Alignment: Race, Party Transformation, and the Rise of Donald Trump* (New Haven, CT: Yale University Press, 2018); Julian E. Zelizer, *The Presidency of Donald J. Trump: A First Historical Assessment* (Princeton, NJ: Princeton University Press, 2022), 98, 145, 175.

19. Joseph W. Campbell, "The 'Close Race That Never Happened': Miscalling the 1980 Election," in *Lost in a Gallup: Polling Failure in U.S. Presidential Elections* (Berkeley: University of California Press, 2020), 108–30.

20. Jonathan Alter, *His Very Best: Jimmy Carter, a Life* (New York: Simon & Schuster, 2021). See also Diane J. Heith, *Polling to Govern: Public Opinion and Presidential Leadership* (Palo Alto, CA: Stanford University Press, 2003), 101.

21. David Farber, *Taken Hostage: The Iran Hostage Crisis and America's First Encounter with Radical Islam* (Princeton, NJ: Princeton University Press, 2006).

22. Michael Schaller, *Ronald Reagan* (New York: Oxford University Press, 2011), 32.

23. Michael Schaller, *Ronald Reagan*, 32.

24. White, *The Values Divide*, 64.

25. Campbell, "The 'Close Race that Never Happened,'" in *Lost in a Gallup*, 108–30.

26. Janet Box-Steffensmeier, Micah Dillard, David Kimball, and William Massengill, "The Long and Short of It: The Unpredictability of Late Deciding Voters," *Electoral Studies* 39 (2015): 185.

27. Remarks by President Joe Biden at a Democratic National Committee Event, October 24, 2022, available at whitehouse.gov.

Chapter 2

1. United States Census Bureau, "Historical Census of Housing Tables: Telephones," 2000, https://www.census.gov/data/tables/time-series/dec/coh-phone.html (accessed January 2023).

2. John Zogby, "By the Numbers: Polling's Future," *Campaigns and Elections*, August 23, 2010.

3. Courtney Kennedy and Hannah Hartig, "Response Rates in Telephone Surveys Have Resumed Their Decline," Pew Research Center, February 27, 2019.

4. Elizabeth Weinstein and Carl Bialik, "Pollsters Debate Merits of Phone, Online Survey," *Wall Street Journal Online*, June 17, 2004. For an example of the poll and a description of the Zogby methodology, see "Battlegrounds States Poll," *Wall Street Journal*, August 2, 2004.

5. Pew Research Center, "Internet/Broadband Fact Sheet," April 7, 2021.

6. Digital Cooperation, "2022 Internet Use Statistics and Data," 2022.

7. For example, Leonie Huddy, Joshua Billig, John Bracciodieta, Lois Hoeffler, Patrick J. Moynihan, and Patricia Pugliani, "The Effect of Interviewer Gender on the Survey Response," *Political Behavior* 19, no. 3 (1997): 197–220, found that there was an effect of the interviewer's gender on a respondents' answers to questions relating to women's concerns.

8. Anthony Rentsch, Brian F. Schaffner, and Justin H. Gross, "The Elusive Likely Voter: Improving Electoral Predictions with More Informed Vote-Propensity Models," *Public Opinion Quarterly* 83, no. 4 (2019): 782–804.

9. Scott Keeter, Nick Hatley, Courtney Kennedy, and Arnold Lau, "What Low Response Rates Mean for Telephone Surveys," Pew Research Center, May 15, 2017.

10. John Zogby, *We Are Many, We Are One: Neo-Tribes and Tribal Analytics in 21st Century America* (New York: Paramount, 2016), 192.

11. Kathleen Donovan, Paul M. Kellstedt, Ellen M. Key, and Matthew J. Lebo, "Motivated Reasoning, Public Opinion, and Presidential Approval," *Political Behavior* 42 (2020): 1201–21. See also Matthew J. Lebo and Daniel Cassino, "The Aggregated Consequences of Motivated Reasoning and the Dynamics of Partisan Presidential Approval," *Political Psychology* 28, no. 6 (2007): 719–46.

12. This model follows the traditional idea of retrospective voting. See Morris P. Fiorina, *Retrospective Voting in American National Elections* (New Haven, CT: Yale University Press, 1981).

13. Alan I. Abramowitz, "Just Weight! The Case for Dynamic Party Identification Weighting," *PS: Political Science & Politics* 39, no. 3 (July 2006): 473–75. This article mentions my method and discusses Republican voting. For further and more detailed discussion of this view of party identification, see Donald Green, Bradley Palmquist, and Eric Schickler, *Partisan Hearts and Minds: Political Parties and the Social Identities of Voters* (New Haven, CT: Yale University Press, 2002).

14. Zogby, *We Are Many, We Are One*.

Chapter 3

1. Mario M. Cuomo, "A Case for the Democrats, 1984: A Tale of Two Cities," keynote address, Democratic National Convention, San Francisco, California, July 16, 1984; included in Richard D. Heffner, Alexander B. Heffner, *A Documentary History of the United States*, 5th ed. (New York: Penguin, 1991), 407–15. See also Robert S. McElvaine, *Mario Cuomo: A Biography* (New York: Scribner, 1988), 344–50.

2. Jon R. Sorensen, "Poll Shows Pataki Overtaking Cuomo Lead of 40 Percent to 35 Percent Is First Statewide Indication of GOP Advantage," *Buffalo News*, June 29, 1994, A7.

3. Sorensen, "Poll Shows Pataki Overtaking Cuomo."

4. Kevin Sack, "The 1994 Campaign: New York Governor; In Cuomo Strategy, Black Voters Are Vital in Struggle for Survival," *New York Times*, October 4, 1994, A1; Todd Purdum, "As State Split, High Turnout Upstate Elected Pataki and Reflected Change," *New York Times*, November 10, 1994, B14.

5. Herbert L. Abrams and Richard Brody, "Bob Dole's Age and Health in the 1996 Election: Did the Media Let Us Down?" *Political Science Quarterly* 113, no. 3 (Fall 1998): 471–91; Howard Kurtz, "Bob Dole's Pollbearers," *Washington Post*, September 10, 1996.

6. Warren J. Mitofsky, "Was 1996 a Worse Year for Polls than 1948?" *The Public Opinion Quarterly* 62, no. 2 (1998): 230–49.

7. Mitofsky, "Was 1996 a Worse Year?"

8. "Proceedings of the Fifty-Second Annual Conference of the American Association for Public Opinion Research," *Public Opinion Quarterly* 61, no. 3 (November 1997): 519–21.

9. Everett Carll Ladd, "The Pollsters' Waterloo," *Wall Street Journal*, November 19, 1996. See also Richard Morin, "Election '96: Winners and Losers," *Washington Post*, November 10, 1996, for his quote, "ALL HAIL Zogby, the pollster who conquered the 1996 election."

10. This article mentions my method and discusses Republican voting. Alan I. Abramowitz, "Just Weight! The Case for Dynamic Party Identification Weighting," *PS: Political Science & Politics* 39, no. 3 (July 2006): 473–75. See also Green, Palmquist, and Schickler, *Partisan Hearts and Minds*. This trend has also persisted in another article in which I am cited: Joshua D. Clinton, John S. Lapinski, and Marc J. Trussler, "Reluctant Republicans, Eager Democrats? Partisan Nonresponse and the Accuracy of 2020 Presidential Pre-election Telephone Polls," *Public Opinion Quarterly* 86, no. 2 (2022): 247–69.

11. Olena Kaminska and Christopher Barnes, "Party Identification Weighting: Experiments to Improve Survey Quality," in *Elections and Exit Polling*, ed. F. J. Scheuren and W. Alvey (Hoboken, NJ: John Wiley and Sons, 2008), 51–61. See also the recent book by G. Elliott Morris, *Strength in Numbers: How Polls Work and Why We Need Them* (New York: W. W. Norton, 2022).

12. "Proceedings of the Fifty-Second Annual Conference of the American Association for Public Opinion Research."

13. "New Jersey: Zogby Poll Shows Movement for the Torch," *The Hotline (National Journal)*, November 4, 1996.

14. Richard L. Berke, "Pre-election Polls; The Surveys Were Accurate, with Some Key Exceptions," *New York Times*, November 8, 1990.

15. Eagleton Institute of Politics, Rutgers University, 1993 archives.

16. Karla Dauler, "Pundits Still Ponder Why Florio Lost," *New York Times*, November 14, 1993.

17. Brett Pulley, "The 1997 Elections: The Overview; In Feverish Last Days, Whitman and McGreevey Appeal to Core Voters," *New York Times*, November 3, 1997.

18. J. David Gopoian and Sissie Hadjiharalambous, "Late-Deciding Voters in Presidential Elections," *Political Behavior* (1994): 55–78. See also Janet Box-Steffensmeier, Micah Dillard, David Kimball, and William Massengill, "The Long and Short of It: The Unpredictability of Late Deciding Voters," *Electoral Studies* 39 (2015): 185.

19. Matthew Hindman, "The Real Lessons of Howard Dean: Reflections on the First Digital Campaign," *Perspectives on Politics* 3, no. 1 (2005): 121–28.

20. David Karol and Edward Miguel, "The Electoral Cost of War: Iraq Casualties and the 2004 US Presidential Election," *Journal of Politics* 69, no. 3 (2007): 633–48.

21. Lester Holt and Chris Matthews, anchors, "Tight Race in the Iowa Caucuses," *NBC News Transcripts Today*, January 19, 2004.

22. Barbara Norrander, "The Attrition Game: Initial Resources, Initial Contests and the Exit of Candidates during the US Presidential Primary Season," *British Journal of Political Science* 36, no. 3 (2006): 487–507.

23. John Oddo, "Creatures of Politics: Media, Message, and the American Presidency," *Presidential Studies Quarterly* 44, no. 1 (March 2014): 193–95. See also "Dean Scream Becomes Online Hit," *BBC News*, January 23, 2004.

24. John Sides and Lynn Vavreck, *The Gamble: Choice and Chance in the 2012 Presidential Election* (Princeton, NJ: Princeton University Press, 2013).

25. Sides and Vavreck, *The Gamble*, 155–61.

26. John Zogby, "Libertarian Leanings of Young Voters Dampen Obama's Appeal," *Forbes*, May 2, 2012. See also CIRCLE (The Center for Information and Research on Civic Learning and Engagement), "Election Night 2012: Half of Young People Voted, 60 Percent Backed President Obama," 2012. This source compares the 2008 and 2012 election results by age group. Cf. CIRCLE, "New Census Data Confirm Increase in Youth Voter Turnout in 2008 Election," 2009.

27. Pew Research Center, "The Generation Gap and the 2012 Election Overview," November 3, 2011.

28. John Zogby, "New *Washington Times*/Zogby Poll: President Leads by 3; But Voters Give Mixed Messages," *Forbes*, October 22, 2012.

29. John Zogby, "What If It's Not Close After All?" *Forbes*, November 4, 2012.

30. Federal Election Commission, "Federal Elections 2012: Election Results for the U.S. President, the U.S. Senate and the U.S. House of Representatives," July 2013, 5; CNN Exit Poll, 2012.

31. CIRCLE, "The Youth Vote in 2012 and the Role of Young Women," May 21, 2013.

Chapter 4

1. Tina Burrett, "Russian State Television Coverage of the 2016 U.S. Presidential Election," *Demokratizatsiya* 26, no. 3 (Summer 2018): 287–319.

2. Courtney Kennedy, Mark Blumenthal, Scott Clement, Joshua D. Clinton, Claire Durand, Charles Franklin, Kyley McGeeney, Lee Miringoff, Kristen Olson, Douglas

Rivers, Lydia Saad, G. Evans Witt, and Christopher Wlezien, "An Evaluation of the 2016 Election Polls in the United States," *Public Opinion Quarterly* 82, no. 1 (Spring 2018): 1–33.

3. Jesse H. Rhodes, Elizabeth Sharrow, Jill Greenlee, and Tatishe Nteta, "Just Locker Room Talk? Explicit Sexism and the Impact of the *Access Hollywood* Tape on Electoral Support for Donald Trump in 2016," *Political Communication* 37, no. 6 (2020): 741–67.

4. Hillary Rodham Clinton, *What Happened* (New York: Simon & Schuster, 2017), 403.

5. Throughout the campaign emails would be heavily associated with the Clinton campaign. In contrast, what voters associated with the Trump campaign kept changing as new issues arrived. See Leticia Bode, Ceren Budak, Jonathan M. Ladd, Frank Newport, Josh Pasek, Lisa O. Singh, Stuart N. Soroka, and Michael W. Traugott, *Words that Matter: How the News and Social Media Shaped the 2016 Presidential Campaign* (Washington, DC: Brookings Institution Press, 2019).

6. According to Real Clear Politics data.

7. CIRCLE, "The Youth Vote in 2012 and the Role of Young Women," May 21, 2013.

8. National Election Pool (ABC News, Associated Press, CBS News, CNN, Fox News, NBC News), National Election Pool Poll # 2008-NATELEC: National Election Day Exit Poll, Edison Media Research/Mitofsky International (Ithaca, NY: Roper Center for Public Opinion Research, Cornell University, 2008).

9. National Election Pool (ABC News, Associated Press, CBS News, CNN, Fox News, NBC News), National Election Pool Poll # 2012-NATELEC: National Election Day Exit Poll, Edison Media Research (Ithaca, NY: Roper Center for Public Opinion Research, Cornell University, 2012).

10. LaGina Gause, "Trump and African American Voters," *Journal of Race, Ethnicity and Politics* 3, no. 1 (2018): 254–56. See also US Census Bureau, "Voter Turnout Rates Among Black Voters, by Age, in U.S. Presidential Elections from 1964 to 2020," *Statista*, November 30, 2021.

11. Roper Center for Public Opinion Research, "How Groups Voted in 2016," collected by Edison Research for the National Election Pool (ABC News, the Associated Press, CBS News, CNN, Fox News and NBC News). See also John Zogby, "A Note to Nate," *Huffington Post*, July 6, 2010.

12. John Sides, "Which Was the Most Accurate National Poll in the 2016 Presidential Election?" *Washington Post*, December 5, 2016; Elizabeth Kolbert, "Senator Pothole," *New York Times*, October 27, 1991.

13. John Zogby, "Caution Abounds on Day of Presidential Race," *Forbes*, November 8, 2016. See also John Zogby, "Hillary Clinton Lost but Obama Coalition Is Alive," *Forbes*, November 14, 2016.

14. John Zogby, "The Wrong Woman at the Wrong Time," *Forbes*, November 9, 2016.

15. Tyler T. Reny and Benjamin J. Newman, "The Opinion-Mobilizing Effect of Social Protest Against Police Violence: Evidence from the 2020 George Floyd Protests," *American Political Science Review* 115, no. 4 (November 2021): 1499–1507.

16. Kimberlé Williams Crenshaw, "Twenty Years of Critical Race Theory: Looking Back to Move Forward," *Connecticut Law Review* 43, no. 5 (2011). See also Richard Delgado and Jean Stefancic, *Critical Race Theory: An Introduction* (New York: NYU Press, 2017).

17. Nikole Hannah-Jones, Caitlin Roper, Ilena Silverman, and Jake Silverstein, *The 1619 Project: A New Origin Story* (New York: One World, 2021).

18. Lisa Lerer, "The Unlikely Issue Shaping the Virginia Governor's Race: Schools," *New York Times*, October 12, 2021.

19. Eric Lach, "Why Was the New Jersey Gubernatorial Race So Close? A Pollster for Governor Phil Murphy Explains How Republicans Nearly Pulled Off an Upset in the Garden State," *New Yorker*, November 26, 2021, quoted from *Bergen County Record*.

20. Patrick Murray, "Pollster: 'I Blew It.' Maybe It's Time to Get Rid of Election Polls," *NJ.com*, November 4, 2021.

21. For background on what pollsters may mean when we refer to "suburban women" and how it changes, see Susan J. Carroll, Richard L. Fox, and Kelly Dittmar, *Gender and Elections*, 5th ed. (New York: Cambridge University Press, 2021), 147. See also David Siders, Sean McMinn, Brakkton Booker, and Jesús A. Rodríguez, "How Black Voters Are Transforming the Suburbs—And American Politics," *Politico*, December 23, 2022. For earlier background on the concept to note the transitions, see Danielle Kurtzleben, "What We Mean When We Talk about 'Suburban Women Voters,'" National Public Radio, *Weekend Edition Saturday*, April 7, 2018.

22. Geoffrey Skelley and Nathaniel Rakich, "Why the President's Party Almost Always Has a Bad Midterm," *FiveThirtyEight*, March 1, 2022. Political scientists have a number of theories for why this is the case. See Robert S. Erikson, "The Puzzle of Midterm Loss," *Journal of Politics* 50, no. 4 (1988): 1011–29. See also James E. Campbell, "Explaining Presidential Losses in Midterm Congressional Elections," *Journal of Politics* 47, no. 4 (1985): 1140–57.

23. Katherine Schaeffer and Ted Van Green, "Key Facts about US Voter Priorities Ahead of the 2022 Midterm Elections," Pew Research Center, 2022.

24. Pew Research Center, "Midterm Voting Intentions Are Divided, Economic Gloom Persists," October 2022, found that only 23 percent of registered voters thought Republicans had done extremely or very well at explaining their plans. Nineteen percent of registered voters thought the same about Democrats.

25. David Weigel, "On the Campaign Trail, Many Republicans Talk of Violence: In Both Swing States and Safe Seats, GOP Candidates Say that Liberals Hate Them Personally and May Turn Rioters or a Police State on People Who Disobey Them," *Washington Post*, July 23, 2022.

26. Michael W. Flamm, *Law and Order: Street Crime, Civil Unrest, and the Crisis of Liberalism in the 1960s* (New York: Columbia University Press, 2005). Even when these policies are race neutral, they serve as racially coded messages that make white respondents think about Black offenders. See Mark Peffley and Jon Hurwitz, "The Racial Components of 'Race-Neutral' Crime Policy Attitudes," *Political Psychology* 23, no. 1 (2002): 59–75.

27. Mary Ziegler, *Roe: The History of a National Obsession* (New Haven, CT: Yale University Press, 2023). See also Mary Ziegler, *Abortion and the Law in America:* Roe v. Wade *to the Present* (New York: Cambridge University Press, 2020).

28. George J. Annas and Elias Sherman, "Thalidomide and the *Titanic*: Reconstructing the Technology Tragedies of the Twentieth Century," *American Journal of Public Health* 89, no. 1 (January 1999): 98–101.

29. Christina Wolbrecht, *The Politics of Women's Rights: Parties, Positions, and Change* (Princeton, NJ: Princeton University Press, 2000).

30. Elizabeth Adell Cook, Ted G. Jelen, and Clyde Wilcox, *Between Two Absolutes: Public Opinion and the Politics of Abortion* (Boulder: Westview Press, 1992).

31. Wolbrecht, *The Politics of Women's Rights.*

32. William J. Clinton, "Statement on the Murder of Dr. Barnett Slepian," *Weekly Compilation of Presidential Documents*, November 2, 1998, 2124–25.

33. Amy Waldman, "Killing of Doctor Becomes a Factor in Political Races," *New York Times*, October 27, 1998.

34. Deborah Tannen, "Let Them Eat Words," *American Prospect*, September 2003, 29–31; Frank Luntz, *Words that Work: It's Not What You Say, It's What People Hear* (London: Hachette, 2007).

35. Ronald M. Peters Jr. and Cindy Simon Rosenthal, *Speaker Nancy Pelosi and the New American Politics* (New York: Oxford University Press, 2010), 136. This book discusses how Luntz's rhetoric, such as partial-birth abortion, challenged Nancy Pelosi's tenure as speaker.

36. Stephen Jessee, Neil Malhotra, and Maya Sen, "A Decade-Long Longitudinal Survey Shows that the Supreme Court Is Now Much More Conservative than the Public," *Proceedings of the National Academy of Sciences* 119, no. 24 (2022).

37. Stephanie Perry, Daniel Arkin, Patrick J. Egan, Hannah Hartig, Courtney Kennedy, and Mara Ostfeld, "Inflation and Abortion Lead the List of Voter Concerns, Edging Out Crime, NBC News Exit Poll Finds," NBC News, November 8, 2022.

38. Jeremy Zogby, "Independents in Battle Ground States Prefer Republicans on Key Issues, but Prefer Democratic Candidates; Claims of Election Fraud Appear to Be Working Against GOP," John Zogby Strategies, 2022.

39. Edison Research, "National Election Pool Exit Polls," National Election Pool (ABC, CBS, CNN, NBC), November 8, 2022. See also Elaine Kamarck and William A. Galston, "It Wasn't Just 'The Economy Stupid'—It Was Abortion," *Brookings Institution Fixgov* (blog), November 10, 2022.

40. Edison Research, "National Election Pool Exit Polls."

41. Edison Research, "National Election Pool Exit Polls."

42. Andrew Prokop, "Why the Red Wave Didn't Come," *Vox*, November 9, 2022; Nicole Narea, "The Guy Who Got the Midterms Right Explains What the Media Got Wrong," *Vox*, November 27, 2022.

Chapter 5

1. John Zogby, "The Dramatic Transformation of NASCAR America," *Forbes*, August 16, 2015.

2. John Zogby, *The Way We'll Be: The Zogby Report on the Transformation of the American Dream* (New York: Random House, 2008).

3. John Zogby, "The Weekly Wal-Mart Shopper: Democrat or Republican?" *Forbes*, August 14, 2015.

4. Zogby, *The Way We'll Be*, 7–10.

5. John Zogby, "A Real Race: McCain vs. Bradley," *New York Times*, January 19, 2000; Mike Allen, "Bradley Tries to Close in on Gore," *Washington Post*, January 31, 2000.

6. To better understand independents, see Samara Klar and Yanna Krupnikov, *Independent Politics: How American Disdain for Parties Leads to Political Inaction* (New York: Cambridge University Press, 2016).

7. Zogby, "A Real Race: McCain and Bradley."

8. Zogby, *We Are Many, We Are One*.

Chapter 6

1. John Zogby, "A Note to Nate," *Huffington Post*, July 6, 2010.

2. G. Elliott Morris, "The Philosophical and Empirical Cases for Ignoring Bad or Biased Pollsters," *Politics by the Numbers*, Substack, February 26, 2023.

3. AAPOR's autopsy of the 2016 polling found little evidence of "shy Trump" voters in 2016. See Courtney Kennedy, Mark Blumenthal, Scott Clement, Joshua D. Clinton, Claire Durand, Charles Franklin, Kyley McGeeney, Lee Miringoff, Kristen Olson, Douglas Rivers, Lydia Saad, G. Evans Witt, and Christopher Wlezien, "An Evaluation of the 2016 Election Polls in the United States," *Public Opinion Quarterly* 82, no. 1 (2018): 1–33.

4. For an excellent review of this Republican strategy, see Jim Rutenberg, Ken Bensinger, and Steve Eder, "The 'Red Wave' Washout: How Skewed Polls Fed a False Election Narrative," *New York Times*, December 31, 2022.

5. Sandy Fitzgerald, "Jim McLaughlin to Newsmax: Dem Pollsters Skewing Results," *Newsmax*, November 2, 2022.

Chapter 7

1. Ben Davis and the *artnet news* staff, "9 of the Absolute Worst Artworks of 2018, as Chosen by the *artnet news* Staff," *artnet news*, December 25, 2018. The painting also sold for $115 million in 2018.

2. Elizabeth Kolbert, "Senator Pothole," *New York Times*, October 27, 1991.

3. Adam Nagourney, "Schumer and D'Amato Waste No Time in Attacking," *New York Times*, September 17, 1998.

4. Adam Nagourney, "Strategy for Senate Race: Get Out the Vote, Selectively," *New York Times*, November 1, 2000.

5. Scott Keeter and Ruth Igielnik, "Can Likely Voter Models Be Improved? Evidence from the 2014 U.S. House Elections," Pew Research Center, January 7, 2016.

6. "General Election: Bush vs. Kerry," RealClearPolitics, November 3, 2004.

7. My polling on this gained national attention. See Jonah Goldberg, "The Beer Test," *National Review*, February 21, 2007. See also Jose Marichal, C. N. Le, Joe Feagin, Jessie Daniels, and Ron Anderson, "Exchange: *Contexts* Bloggers on Politics," *Contexts* 7, no. 4 (Fall 2008): 12–15.

8. Patrick J. Egan, *Partisan Priorities: How Issue Ownership Drives and Distorts American Politics* (New York: Cambridge University Press, 2013).

9. John Kenneth White and John J. Zogby, "The Likeable Partisan: George W. Bush and the Transformation of the American Presidency," in *High Risk and Big Ambition: Presidency of George W. Bush*, ed. Steven E. Scheir (Pittsburgh: University of Pittsburgh Press, 2004), 79–96.

10. Gert Stulp, Abraham P. Buunk, Simon Verhulst, and Thomas V. Pollet, "Tall Claims? Sense and Nonsense about the Importance of the Height of US Presidents," *Leadership Quarterly* 24, no. 1 (2013): 159–71.

11. Richard Morin and Claudia Deane, "Report Acknowledges Inaccuracies in 2004 Exit Polls," *Washington Post*, January 20, 2005.

12. Robert F. Kennedy Jr., "Was the 2004 Election Stolen?" *Rolling Stone*, June 16, 2006.

13. Jennifer L. Lawless, "Sexism and Gender Bias in Election 2008: A More Complex Path for Women in Politics," *Politics & Gender* 5, no. 1 (2009): 70–80. See also Hendrik Hertzberg, "Second Those Emotions: Hillary's Tears," *New Yorker*, January 13, 2008.

14. Kenneth F. Bunting, "Momentum Fleeting and Illusory," *SFGate*, January 14, 2008.

15. Don Frederick, "Opinion: Missing the Outcome in California," *Los Angeles Times*, February 6, 2008.

16. Carl Bialik, "Election Handicappers Are Using Risky Tool: Mixed Poll Averages," *Wall Street Journal*, February 15, 2008.

Chapter 8

1. "2001 Presidential Election," *Iran Social Science Data Portal*, funded by the Social Science Research Council, Princeton University and Syracuse University, 2001.

2. John Zogby, "What Iranians Want," *Forbes*, June 25, 2009.

3. Abbas Amanat, *Iran: A Modern History* (New Haven, CT: Yale University Press, 2017).

4. Amanat, *Iran: A Modern History*.

5. Jo Tuckman, *Mexico: Democracy Interrupted* (New Haven, CT: Yale University Press, 2012).

6. Antonio Ugues Jr., "Public Perceptions of Clean Elections in Mexico: An Analysis of the 2000, 2006, and 2012 Elections," *Journal of Politics in Latin America* 10, no. 2 (2018): 77–98.

7. Marcela Szymanski, "Observing the 2000 Mexico Elections," Carter Center, March 2001.

8. Jorge I. Domínguez and Chappell H. Lawson, *Mexico's Pivotal Democratic Election: Candidates, Voters, and the Presidential Campaign of 2000* (Palo Alto, CA: Stanford University Press, 2004).

9. Gordon Robertson, "Mexican Presidential Race Is Shaping Up Between Labastida and Fox," *CNN International World News*, April 26, 2000.

10. Brandon Rottinghaus and Irina Alberro, "Rivaling the PRI: The Image Management of Vicente Fox and the Use of Public Opinion Polling in the 2000 Mexican Election," *Latin American Politics and Society*, December 19, 2008.

11. Adam Tanner, "Exit Polls See Albania's Ruling Democrats Winning," Reuters, June 28, 2009.

12. John Zogby, "Polling the Albanian Election," *Forbes*, July 9, 2009.

13. Robert Langkjaer-Bain, "Albanian Election Poll Heralds 'New Era' for Research, Says Zogby," *Research Live*, July 10, 2009.

14. This book chapter discusses some of my findings on social media use: Pippa Norris, "Political Mobilization and Social Networks: The Example of the Arab Spring," in *Electronic Democracy*, ed. Norbert Kersting, Michael Stein, and John Trent (New York: Columbia University Press/Verlag Barbara Budrich, 2012), 53–76.

15. Emma C. Murphy, "The Tunisian Elections of October 2011: A Democratic Consensus," *Journal of North African Studies* 18, no. 2 (2013): 231–47.

16. Ibrahim Fraihat, *Unfinished Revolutions: Yemen, Libya, and Tunisia after the Arab Spring* (New Haven, CT: Yale University Press, 2016).

17. This article uses my polling data, in conjunction with my brother Jim, to better understand Arab nations: Peter A. Furia and Russell E. Lucas, "Determinants of Arab Public Opinion on Foreign Relations," *International Studies Quarterly* 50, no. 3 (2006): 585–605.

18. Marcus Buckingham and Curt Coffman, *First, Break All the Rules: What the World's Greatest Managers Do Differently* (New York: Gallup Press, 2016).

Chapter 9

1. Jacob Bronowski, writer and producer, *The Ascent of Man*, BBC and Time-Life Films, 1973.

2. Robert G. Turnbull, *Interpretative Chapters on the Timaeus, the Theaetetus, the Sophist, and the Philebus* (Toronto: University of Toronto Press), 11–14.

3. Aline Kraditor, *"Jimmy Higgins": The Mental World of the American Rank-and-File Communist, 1930–1958* (Westport, CT: Praeger, 1988).

4. William Lederer and Eugene Burdick, *The Ugly American* (New York: Norton, 1958); Eugene Burdick, *The 480: A Novel of Politics* (New York: McGraw-Hill, 1964).

Works Cited

Academic Journals

Abramowitz, Alan. "Just Weight! The Case for Dynamic Party Identification Weighting." *PS: Political Science & Politics* 39, no. 3 (July 2006): 473–75. This article mentions my method and discusses Republican voting.

Abrams, Herbert, and Richard Brody. "Bob Dole's Age and Health in the 1996 Election: Did the Media Let Us Down?" *Political Science Quarterly* 113, no. 3 (Fall 1998): 471–91.

Annas, George, and Elias Sherman. "Thalidomide and the *Titanic*: Reconstructing the Technology Tragedies of the Twentieth Century." *American Journal of Public Health* 89, no. 1 (January 1999): 98–101.

Box-Steffensmeier, Janet, Suzanna De Boef, and Tse-Min Lin. "The Dynamics of the Partisan Gender Gap." *American Political Science Review* 98, no. 3 (2004): 515–28.

Box-Steffensmeier, Janet, Micah Dillard, David Kimball, and William Massengill. "The Long and Short of It: The Unpredictability of Late Deciding Voters." *Electoral Studies* 39 (2015): 185.

Bracy, Henry, Michael C. Herron, Walter R. Mebane Jr., and Jasjeet Singh Sekhon. "Law and Data: The Butterfly Ballot Episode." *PS: Political Science & Politics* 34, no. 1 (2001): 64.

Burrett, Tina. "Russian State Television Coverage of the 2016 U.S. Presidential Election." *Demokratizatsiya* 26, no. 3 (Summer 2018): 287–319.

Campbell, James. "Explaining Presidential Losses in Midterm Congressional Elections." *Journal of Politics* 47, no. 4 (1985): 1140–57.

Clinton, Joshua, John S. Lapinski, and Marc J. Trussler. "Reluctant Republicans, Eager Democrats? Partisan Nonresponse and the Accuracy of 2020 Presidential Pre-election Telephone Polls." *Public Opinion Quarterly* 86, no. 2 (2022): 247–69.

Crenshaw, Kimberlé Williams. "Twenty Years of Critical Race Theory: Looking Back to Move Forward." *Connecticut Law Review* 43, no. 5 (2011).

Donovan, Kathleen, Paul M. Kellstedt, Ellen M. Key, and Matthew J. Lebo. "Motivated Reasoning, Public Opinion, and Presidential Approval." *Political Behavior* 42 (2020): 1201–21.

Erikson, Robert. "The Puzzle of Midterm Loss." *Journal of Politics* 50, no. 4 (1988): 1011–29.

Furia, Peter, and Russell E. Lucas. "Determinants of Arab Public Opinion on Foreign Relations." *International Studies Quarterly* 50, no. 3 (2006): 585–605.

Gause, LaGina. "Trump and African American Voters." *Journal of Race, Ethnicity and Politics* 3, no. 1 (2018): 254–56.

Gopoian, David, and Sissie Hadjiharalambous. "Late-Deciding Voters in Presidential Elections." *Political Behavior* (1994): 55–78.

Hindman, Matthew. "The Real Lessons of Howard Dean: Reflections on the First Digital Campaign." *Perspectives on Politics* 3, no. 1 (2005): 121–28.

Huddy, Leonie, Joshua Billig, John Bracciodieta, Lois Hoeffler, Patrick J. Moynihan, and Patricia Pugliani. "The Effect of Interviewer Gender on the Survey Response." *Political Behavior* 19, no. 3 (1997): 197–220.

Jessee, Stephen, Neil Malhotra, and Maya Sen. "A Decade-Long Longitudinal Survey Shows that the Supreme Court Is Now Much More Conservative than the Public." *Proceedings of the National Academy of Sciences* 119, no. 24 (2022).

Karol, David, and Edward Miguel. "The Electoral Cost of War: Iraq Casualties and the 2004 US Presidential Election." *Journal of Politics* 69, no. 3 (2007): 633–48.

Kennedy, Courtney, Mark Blumenthal, Scott Clement, Joshua D. Clinton, Claire Durand, Charles Franklin, Kyley McGeeney, Lee Miringoff, Kristen Olson, Douglas Rivers, Lydia Saad, G. Evans Witt, and Christopher Wlezien. "An Evaluation of the 2016 Election Polls in the United States." *Public Opinion Quarterly* 82, no. 1 (Spring 2018): 1–33.

Lawless, Jennifer. "Sexism and Gender Bias in Election 2008: A More Complex Path for Women in Politics." *Politics & Gender* 5, no. 1 (2009): 70–80.

Lebo, Matthew, and Daniel Cassino. "The Aggregated Consequences of Motivated Reasoning and the Dynamics of Partisan Presidential Approval." *Political Psychology* 28, no. 6 (2007): 719–46.

Marichal, Jose, C. N. Le, Joe Feagin, Jessie Daniels, and Ron Anderson. "Exchange: *Contexts* Bloggers on Politics." *Contexts* 7, no. 4 (Fall 2008): 12–15.

Mitofsky, Warren. "Was 1996 a Worse Year for Polls than 1948?" *Public Opinion Quarterly* 62, no. 2 (1998): 230–49.

Murphy, Emma. "The Tunisian Elections of October 2011: A Democratic Consensus." *Journal of North African Studies* 18, no. 2 (2013): 231–47.

Mutz, Diana. "Effects of Horse-Race Coverage on Campaign Coffers: Strategic Contributing in Presidential Primaries." *Journal of Politics* 57, no. 4 (1995): 1015–42.

Norrander, Barbara. "The Attrition Game: Initial Resources, Initial Contests and the Exit of Candidates during the US Presidential Primary Season." *British Journal of Political Science* 36, no. 3 (2006): 487–507.

Oddo, John. "Creatures of Politics: Media, Message, and the American Presidency." *Presidential Studies Quarterly* 44, no. 1 (March 2014): 193–95.

Patterson, Thomas. "Of Polls, Mountains: US Journalists and Their Use of Election Surveys." *Public Opinion Quarterly* 69, no. 5 (2005): 716–24.

Peffley, Mark, and Jon Hurwitz. "The Racial Components of 'Race-Neutral' Crime Policy Attitudes." *Political Psychology* 23, no. 1 (2002): 59–75.

"Proceedings of the Fifty-Second Annual Conference of the American Association for Public Opinion Research." *Public Opinion Quarterly* 61, no. 3 (November 1997): 519–21.

Rentsch, Anthony, Brian F. Schaffner, and Justin H. Gross. "The Elusive Likely Voter: Improving Electoral Predictions with More Informed Vote-Propensity Models." *Public Opinion Quarterly* 83, no. 4 (2019): 782–804.

Reny, Tyler, and Benjamin J. Newman. "The Opinion-Mobilizing Effect of Social Protest Against Police Violence: Evidence from the 2020 George Floyd Protests." *American Political Science Review* 115, no. 4 (November 2021): 1499–1507.

Rhodes, Jesse, Elizabeth Sharrow, Jill Greenlee, and Tatishe Nteta. "Just Locker Room Talk? Explicit Sexism and the Impact of the *Access Hollywood* Tape on Electoral Support for Donald Trump in 2016." *Political Communication* (2020).

Rottinghaus, Brandon, and Irina Alberro. "Rivaling the PRI: The Image Management of Vicente Fox and the Use of Public Opinion Polling in the 2000 Mexican Election." *Latin American Politics and Society*, December 19, 2008.

Stulp, Gert, Abraham P. Buunk, Simon Verhulst, and Thomas V. Pollet. "Tall Claims? Sense and Nonsense about the Importance of the Height of US Presidents." *Leadership Quarterly* 24, no. 1 (2013): 159–71.

Ugues, Antonio, Jr. "Public Perceptions of Clean Elections in Mexico: An Analysis of the 2000, 2006, and 2012 Elections." *Journal of Politics in Latin America* 10, no. 2 (2018): 77–98.

Wand, Jonathan, Kenneth W. Shotts, Jasjeet S. Sekhon, Walter R. Mebane, Michael C. Herron, and Henry E. Brady. "The Butterfly Did It: The Aberrant Vote for Buchanan in Palm Beach County, Florida." *American Political Science Review* 95, no. 4 (2001): 793–810.

Books

Abramowitz, Alan. *The Great Alignment: Race, Party Transformation, and the Rise of Donald Trump* (New Haven, CT: Yale University Press, 2018).

Alter, Jonathan. *His Very Best: Jimmy Carter, a Life* (New York: Simon & Schuster, 2021).

Amanat, Abbas. *Iran: A Modern History* (New Haven, CT: Yale University Press, 2017).

Bode, Leticia, Ceren Budak, Jonathan M. Ladd, Frank Newport, Josh Pasek, Lisa O. Singh, Stuart N. Soroka, and Michael W. Traugott. *Words That Matter: How the News and Social Media Shaped the 2016 Presidential Campaign* (Washington, DC: Brookings Institution Press, 2019).

Buckingham, Marcus, and Curt Coffman. *First, Break All the Rules: What the World's Greatest Managers Do Differently* (New York: Gallup Press, 2016).

Burdick, Eugene. *The 480: A Novel of Politics* (New York: McGraw-Hill, 1964).

Campbell, Joseph. *Lost in a Gallup: Polling Failure in U.S. Presidential Elections* (Berkeley: University of California Press, 2020).

Carroll, Susan, Richard L. Fox, and Kelly Dittmar. *Gender and Elections.* 5th ed. (New York: Cambridge University Press, 2021).

Clinton, Hillary. *What Happened* (New York: Simon & Schuster, 2017).

Cook, Elizabeth Adell, Ted G. Jelen, and Clyde Wilcox. *Between Two Absolutes: Public Opinion and the Politics of Abortion* (Boulder: Westview Press, 1992).

Delgado, Richard, and Jean Stefancic. *Critical Race Theory: An Introduction* (New York: NYU Press, 2017).

Domínguez, Jorge, and Chappell H. Lawson. *Mexico's Pivotal Democratic Election: Candidates, Voters, and the Presidential Campaign of 2000* (Palo Alto, CA: Stanford University Press, 2004).

Egan, Patrick. *Partisan Priorities: How Issue Ownership Drives and Distorts American Politics* (New York: Cambridge University Press, 2013).

Farber, David. *Taken Hostage: The Iran Hostage Crisis and America's First Encounter with Radical Islam* (Princeton, NJ: Princeton University Press, 2006).

Fiorina, Morris. *Retrospective Voting in American National Elections* (New Haven, CT: Yale University Press, 1981).

Flamm, Michael. *Law and Order: Street Crime, Civil Unrest, and the Crisis of Liberalism in the 1960s* (New York: Columbia University Press, 2005).

Fraihat, Ibrahim. *Unfinished Revolutions: Yemen, Libya, and Tunisia after the Arab Spring* (New Haven, CT: Yale University Press, 2016).

Green, Donald, Bradley Palmquist, and Eric Schickler. *Partisan Hearts and Minds: Political Parties and the Social Identities of Voters* (New Haven, CT: Yale University Press, 2002).

Hannah-Jones, Nikole, Caitlin Roper, Ilena Silverman, and Jake Silverstein. *The 1619 Project: A New Origin Story* (New York: One World, 2021).

Hasen, Richard. *The Voting Wars: From Florida 2000 to the Next Election Meltdown* (New Haven, CT: Yale University Press, 2012).

Heffner, Richard, and Alexander B. Heffner. *A Documentary History of the United States.* 5th ed. (New York: Penguin, 1991).

Heith, Diane. *Polling to Govern: Public Opinion and Presidential Leadership* (Palo Alto, CA: Stanford University Press, 2003).

Hudson, Robert. *The New Politics of Old Age Policy* (Baltimore, MD: Johns Hopkins University Press, 2014).

Klar, Samara, and Yanna Krupnikov. *Independent Politics: How American Disdain for Parties Leads to Political Inaction* (New York: Cambridge University Press, 2016).

Kraditor, Aline. *"Jimmy Higgins": The Mental World of the American Rank-and-File Communist, 1930–1958* (Westport, CT: Praeger, 1988).

Lederer, William, and Eugene Burdick. *The Ugly American* (New York: Norton, 1958).

Luntz, Frank. *Words that Work: It's Not What You Say, It's What People Hear* (London: Hachette, 2007).

Mason, Lilliana. *Uncivil Agreement: How Politics Became Our Identity* (Chicago: University of Chicago Press, 2018).

McElvaine, Robert. *Mario Cuomo: A Biography* (New York: Scribner, 1988).

McPherson, James. *Abraham Lincoln* (Oxford: Oxford University Press, 2009).

Morris, G. Elliott. *Strength in Numbers: How Polls Work and Why We Need Them* (New York: W. W. Norton, 2022).

Munger, Kevin. *Generation Gap: Why the Baby Boomers Still Dominate American Politics and Culture* (New York: Columbia University Press, 2022).

Norris, Pippa. "Political Mobilization and Social Networks. The Example of the Arab Spring." In *Electronic Democracy*, edited by Norbert Kersting, Michael Stein, and John Trent, 55–76 (New York: Columbia University Press/Verlag Barbara Budrich, 2012).

Parsons, Lynn Hudson. *The Birth of Modern Politics: Andrew Jackson, John Quincy Adams, and the Election of 1828* (New York: Oxford University Press, 2009).

Peters, Ronald, Jr., and Cindy Simon Rosenthal. *Speaker Nancy Pelosi and the New American Politics* (New York: Oxford University Press, 2010).

Schaller, Michael. *Ronald Reagan* (Oxford: Oxford University Press, 2011).

Scheuren, F. J., and W. Alvey, eds. *Elections and Exit Polling* (Hoboken, NJ: John Wiley and Sons, 2008).

Shafer, Byron, and Richard Johnston. *The End of Southern Exceptionalism: Class, Race, and Partisan Change in the Postwar South* (Cambridge, MA: Harvard University Press, 2009).

Sides, John, and Lynn Vavreck. *The Gamble: Choice and Chance in the 2012 Presidential Election* (Princeton, NJ: Princeton University Press, 2013).

Tuckman, Jo. *Mexico: Democracy Interrupted* (New Haven, CT: Yale University Press, 2012).

Turnbull, Robert. *Interpretative Chapters on the Timaeus, the Theaetetus, the Sophist, and the Philebus* (Toronto: University of Toronto Press, 1998).

White, John Kenneth, with a foreword by John Zogby. *The Values Divide: American Politics and Culture in Transition* (New York: Chatham House, 2003).

White, John Kenneth, and John Zogby. "The Likeable Partisan: George W. Bush and the Transformation of the American Presidency." In *High Risk and Big Ambition: Presidency of George W. Bush*, edited by Steven E. Scheir, 79–96 (Pittsburgh: University of Pittsburgh Press, 2004).

Wolbrecht, Christina. *The Politics of Women's Rights: Parties, Positions, and Change* (Princeton, NJ: Princeton University Press, 2000).

Zelizer, Julian. *The Presidency of Donald J. Trump: A First Historical Assessment* (Princeton, NJ: Princeton University Press, 2022).

Ziegler, Mary. *Abortion and the Law in America:* Roe v. Wade *to the Present* (New York: Cambridge University Press, 2020).

Ziegler, Mary. *Roe: The History of a National Obsession* (New Haven, CT: Yale University Press, 2023).

Zogby, John. *The Way We'll Be: The Zogby Report on the Transformation of the American Dream* (New York: Random House, 2008).

Zogby, John. *We Are Many, We Are One: Neo-Tribes and Tribal Analytics in 21st Century America* (New York: Paramount).

Magazines/Blogs

Goldberg, Jonah. "The Beer Test." *National Review*, February 21, 2007.

Hertzberg, Hendrik. "Second Those Emotions: Hillary's Tears." *New Yorker*, January 13, 2008.

Kamarck, Elaine, and William A. Galston. "It Wasn't Just 'The Economy Stupid'—It Was Abortion." *Brookings Institution Fixgov* (blog), November 10, 2022.

Kennedy, Robert, Jr. "Was the 2004 Election Stolen?" *Rolling Stone*, June 16, 2006.

Lach, Eric. "Why Was the New Jersey Gubernatorial Race So Close? A Pollster for Governor Phil Murphy Explains How Republicans Nearly Pulled Off an Upset in the Garden State." *New Yorker*, November 26, 2021, quoted from *Bergen County Record*.

Morris, G. Elliott. "The Philosophical and Empirical Cases for Ignoring Bad or Biased Pollsters." *Politics by the Numbers*, Substack, February 26, 2023.

Narea, Nicole. "The Guy Who Got the Midterms Right Explains What the Media Got Wrong." *Vox*, November 27, 2022.

Prokop, Andrew. "Why the Red Wave Didn't Come." *Vox*, November 9, 2022.

Siders, David, Sean McMinn, Brakkton Booker, and Jesús A. Rodríguez. "How Black Voters Are Transforming the Suburbs—And American Politics." *Politico*, December 23, 2022.

Tannen, Deborah. "Let Them Eat Words." *American Prospect*, September 2003.

Zogby, John. "By the Numbers: Polling's Future." *Campaigns and Elections*, August 23, 2010.

Zogby, John. "Caution Abounds on Day of Presidential Race." *Forbes*, November 8, 2016.

Zogby, John. "The Dramatic Transformation of NASCAR America." *Forbes*, August 16, 2015.

Zogby, John. "Hillary Clinton Lost but Obama Coalition Is Alive." *Forbes*, November 14, 2016.

Zogby, John. "Libertarian Leanings of Young Voters Dampen Obama's Appeal." *Forbes*, May 2, 2012.

Zogby, John. "New *Washington Times*/Zogby Poll: President Leads by 3; But Voters Give Mixed Messages." *Forbes*, October 22, 2012.

Zogby, John. "A Note to Nate." *Huffington Post*, July 6, 2010.

Zogby, John. "Polling the Albanian Election." *Forbes*, July 9, 2009.

Zogby, John. "The Weekly Wal-Mart Shopper: Democrat or Republican?" *Forbes*, August 14, 2015.

Zogby, John. "What If It's Not Close After All?" *Forbes*, November 4, 2012.

Zogby, John. "What Iranians Want." *Forbes*, June 25, 2009.

Zogby, John. "The Wrong Woman at the Wrong Time." *Forbes*, November 9, 2016.

Newspapers

Allen, Mike. "Bradley Tries to Close in on Gore." *Washington Post*, January 31, 2000.

BBC News. "Dean Scream Becomes Online Hit." January 23, 2004.

Berke, Richard. "Pre-election Polls; The Surveys Were Accurate, with Some Key Exceptions." *New York Times*, November 8, 1990.

Bialik, Carl. "Election Handicappers Are Using Risky Tool: Mixed Poll Averages." *Wall Street Journal*, February 15, 2008.

Bunting, Kenneth. "Momentum Fleeting and Illusory." *SFGate*, January 14, 2008.

Clymer, Adam. "Poll Shows a Married Single Gap in Last Election." *New York Times*, January 6, 1983.

Dauler, Karla. "Pundits Still Ponder Why Florio Lost." *New York Times*, November 14, 1993.

Fitzgerald, Sandy. "Jim McLaughlin to *Newsmax*: Dem Pollsters Skewing Results." *Newsmax*, November 2, 2022.

Frederick, Don. "Opinion: Missing the Outcome in California." *Los Angeles Times*, February 6, 2008.

Holt, Lester, and Chris Matthews, anchors. "Tight Race in the Iowa Caucuses." *NBC News Transcripts Today*, January 19, 2004.

Kolbert, Elizabeth. "Senator Pothole." *New York Times*, October 27, 1991.

Kurtz, Howard. "Bob Dole's Pollbearers." *Washington Post*, September 10, 1996.

Kurtzleben, Danielle. "What We Mean When We Talk about 'Suburban Women Voters.'" National Public Radio, *Weekend Edition Saturday*, April 7, 2018.

Ladd, Everett Carll. "The Pollsters' Waterloo." *Wall Street Journal*, November 19, 1996.

Lerer, Lisa. "The Unlikely Issue Shaping the Virginia Governor's Race: Schools." *New York Times*, October 12, 2021.

Morin, Richard. "Election '96: Winners and Losers." *Washington Post*, November 10, 1996.

Morin, Richard, and Claudia Deane. "Report Acknowledges Inaccuracies in 2004 Exit Polls." *Washington Post*, January 20, 2005.

Murray, Patrick. "Pollster: 'I Blew It.' Maybe It's Time to Get Rid of Election Polls." *NJ.com*, November 4, 2021.

Nagourney, Adam. "Schumer and D'Amato Waste No Time in Attacking." *New York Times*, September 17, 1998.

Nagourney, Adam. "Strategy for Senate Race: Get Out the Vote, Selectively." *New York Times*, November 1, 2000.

Perry, Stephanie, Daniel Arkin, Patrick J. Egan, Hannah Hartig, Courtney Kennedy, and Mara Ostfeld. "Inflation and Abortion Lead the List of Voter Concerns, Edging Out Crime, NBC News Exit Poll Finds." *NBC News*, November 8, 2022.

Pulley, Brent. "The 1997 Elections: The Overview; In Feverish Last Days, Whitman and McGreevey Appeal to Core Voters." *New York Times*, November 3, 1997.

Purdum, Todd. "As State Split, High Turnout Upstate Elected Pataki and Reflected Change." *New York Times*, November 10, 1994.

Robertson, Gordon. "Mexican Presidential Race Is Shaping Up Between Labastida and Fox." *CNN International World News*, April 26, 2000.

Rutenberg, Jim, Ken Bensinger, and Steve Eder. "The 'Red Wave' Washout: How Skewed Polls Fed a False Election Narrative." *New York Times*, December 31, 2022.

Sack, Kevin. "The 1994 Campaign: New York Governor; In Cuomo Strategy, Black Voters Are Vital in Struggle for Survival." *New York Times*, October 4, 1994.

Sides, John. "Which Was the Most Accurate National Poll in the 2016 Presidential Election?" *Washington Post*, December 5, 2016.

Sorensen, Jon. "Poll Shows Pataki Overtaking Cuomo Lead of 40% to 35% Is First Statewide Indication of GOP Advantage." *Buffalo News*, June 29, 1994.

Tanner, Adam. "Exit Polls See Albania's Ruling Democrats Winning." Reuters, June 28, 2009.

Waldman, Amy. "Killing of Doctor Becomes a Factor in Political Races." *New York Times*, October 27, 1998.

Wall Street Journal. "Battlegrounds States Poll." August 2, 2004.

Weigel, David. "On the Campaign Trail, Many Republicans Talk of Violence: In Both Swing States and Safe Seats, GOP Candidates Say that Liberals Hate Them Personally and May Turn Rioters or a Police State on People Who Disobey Them." *Washington Post*, July 23, 2022.

Weinstein, Elizabeth, and Carl Bialik. "Pollsters Debate Merits of Phone, Online Survey." *Wall Street Journal Online*, June 17, 2004.

Zogby, John. "A Real Race: McCain vs. Bradley." *New York Times*, January 19, 2000.

Political Documentation (Polling, Statements, etc.)

The Bulletin's Frontrunner. "Zogby Most Accurate Predictor of Presidential Results." November 9, 2000.

CIRCLE. "Election Night 2012: Half of Young People Voted, 60% Backed President Obama." 2012.

CIRCLE. "New Census Data Confirm Increase in Youth Voter Turnout in 2008 Election." 2009.

CIRCLE. "The Youth Vote in 2012 and the Role of Young Women." May 21, 2013.

Clinton, William. "Statement on the Murder of Dr. Barnett Slepian." *Weekly Compilation of Presidential Documents*, November 2, 1998.

Digital Cooperation. "2022 Internet Use Statistics and Data." 2022.

Eagleton Institute of Politics, Rutgers University, 1993 archives.

Edison Research. "National Election Pool Exit Polls." National Election Pool (ABC, CBS, CNN, NBC), November 8, 2022.

Federal Election Commission. "Federal Elections 2012: Election Results for the U.S. President, the U.S. Senate and the U.S. House of Representatives." July 2013.

The Hotline (National Journal). "New Jersey: Zogby Poll Shows Movement for the Torch." November 4, 1996.

The Hotline (National Journal). "Poll Update—Reuters/Zogby: 60% Say if Gore Wins, He Stole the Election." November 27, 2000.

Iran Social Science Data Portal. "2001 Presidential Election." Funded by the Social Science Research Council, Princeton University and Syracuse University, 2001.

Keeter, Scott, and Ruth Igielnik. "Can Likely Voter Models Be Improved? Evidence from the 2014 U.S. House Elections." Pew Research Center, January 7, 2016.

Keeter, Scott, Nick Hatley, Courtney Kennedy, and Arnold Lau. "What Low Response Rates Mean for Telephone Surveys." Pew Research Center, May 15, 2017.

Kennedy, Courtney, and Hannah Hartig. "Response Rates in Telephone Surveys Have Resumed Their Decline." Pew Research Center, February 27, 2019.

Langkjaer-Bain, Robert. "Albanian Election Poll Heralds 'New Era' for Research, says Zogby." *Research Live*, July 10, 2009.

National Election Pool (ABC News, Associated Press, CBS News, CNN, Fox News, NBC News). National Election Pool Poll # 2008-NATELEC: National Election Day Exit Poll.

National Election Pool (ABC News, Associated Press, CBS News, CNN, Fox News, NBC News). National Election Pool Poll # 2012-NATELEC: National Election Day Exit Poll, Edison Media Research (Ithaca, NY: Roper Center for Public Opinion Research, Cornell University, 2012).

National Election Pool Poll # 2008-NATELEC: National Election Day Exit Poll, Edison Media Research/Mitofsky International (Ithaca, NY: Roper Center for Public Opinion Research, Cornell University, 2008).

Pew Research Center. "The Generation Gap and the 2012 Election Overview." November 3, 2011.

Pew Research Center. "Internet/Broadband Fact Sheet." April 7, 2021.

Pew Research Center. "Midterm Voting Intentions Are Divided, Economic Gloom Persists." October 2022.

RealClearPolitics. "General Election: Bush vs. Kerry." November 3, 2004.

Roper Center for Public Opinion Research. "How Groups Voted in 2016." Collected by Edison Research for the National Election Pool (ABC News, the Associated Press, CBS News, CNN, Fox News and NBC News).

Schaeffer, Katherine, and Ted Van Green. "Key Facts about US Voter Priorities Ahead of the 2022 Midterm Elections." Pew Research Center, 2022.

Skelley, Geoffrey, and Nathaniel Rakich. "Why the President's Party Almost Always Has a Bad Midterm." *FiveThirtyEight*, March 1, 2022.

Szymanski, Marcela. "Observing the 2000 Mexico Elections." The Carter Center, March 2001.

United States Census Bureau. "Historical Census of Housing Tables: Telephones." 2000. https://www.census.gov/data/tables/time-series/dec/coh-phone.html (accessed January 2023).

United States Census Bureau. "Voter Turnout Rates Among Black Voters, by Age, in U.S. Presidential Elections from 1964 to 2020." *Statista*, November 30, 2021.

White House Bulletin. "Bush Up by 5 in MSNBC/Reuters/Zogby Tracking Poll." November 1, 2000.

White House Bulletin. "Bush Up by 3 in MSNBC/Reuters/Zogby Tracking Poll." November 2, 2000.

White House Bulletin. "Gore Ahead by 2 in MSNBC/Reuters/Zogby Tracking Poll." November 7, 2000.

Zogby, Jeremy. "Independents in Battle Ground States Prefer Republicans on Key Issues, But Prefer Democratic Candidates; Claims of Election Fraud Appear to Be Working Against GOP." John Zogby Strategies, 2022.

Index